the Last Enemy

BOOKS IN PRINT BY THE SAME AUTHOR

Israel: Act III
Israel Today
Is God Dead
Riots in the Streets
Man at the Top
The Meaning of Loneliness

the Last Enemy

Richard Wolff

Canon Press
Washington, D.C.

Jacket Picture:

Tombstone in Kenya. At first such tomb "stones" were made out of clay if the deceased was a woman who had been a member of a secret society. The "statue" was usually a rather crude representation of the deceased. Once the clay statue was in place, articles of clothing and other personal belongings which had been the possession of the deceased were hung on the sitting form. Christians used a cross. A syncretism developed which is represented by a picture "half woman" and "half cross." One was anxious to have "insurance" on both sides of the fence.

Permission to use the jacket picture was received from the Basler Mission-Deutscher Zweig e.V., Stuttgart.

ISBN # 0 913686 13 1
Copyright © 1974 by Canon Press
1014 Washington Building
Washington, D.C.
Printed in the United States of America

CONTENTS

I
THE PROBLEM

Much in this world is uncertain, but the fact that we shall die is beyond conjecture. The validity of Benjamin Franklin's observation, "In this world nothing can be said to be certain, except death and taxes," goes without question. While some may be able to avoid taxes, no one can hope to escape death. As Sir Walter Scott put it:

> And come he slow, or come he fast,
> It is but Death who comes at last.
>
> [*Marmion*, II, 30]

Ancient poets lamented the brevity of life:

> Behold, thou has made my days a few handbreadths,
> and my lifetime is as nothing in thy sight.
> Surely every man stands as a mere breath!
>
> [Psalm 39:5]

Pascal observed that between us and heaven or hell there is only life, which is the frailest thing in the world.

But death is far more than a brief, unpleasant moment to be faced sometime in the future; the whole of life stands under its shadow, relentlessly moving toward the boundary. Chaucer expressed it well:

> When I was born, so long ago,
> Death drew the tap of life and let it flow;
> And ever since the tap has done its task,
> And now there's little but an empty cask.
> My stream of life's but drops upon the rim.
>
> [The Reeve's Prologue
> from *The Canterbury Tales*,
> Translated by Nevill Coghill]

1

Death does not lurk threatening in the future; it penetrates present concerns, is part and parcel of life itself. Death cannot be divorced from life and should not be viewed in isolation. It might almost be called a way of life, a mode of existence. Death permeates life. Life and death coexist. Man's mortality does not begin at the moment of death; death is the horizon of life, it is part of the scenery.

Deeply conscious of the presence of death, some have abandoned themselves in despair to nihilism. All is meaningless and absurd, reduced to nothingness and emptiness. This somber outlook makes it difficult to face death and equally difficult to face life, since our view of death determines our philosophy of life.

Many different opinions have been expressed about death ever since the dawn of history. The *Book of the Dead* and the pyramids bear witness to the Egyptians' preoccupation with it. In the Babylonian *Epic of Gilgamesh* death is the central theme. Ancient religious rites are related to death and rebirth. The enigma of death has challenged the mind of man across the ages, given birth to myth, drama, poetry, and inspired philosophy.

What is death? It has become increasingly difficult to determine the boundary between life and death. But aside from the medical and legal problem of definition, what is the meaning of death . . . and of life? Is death separation or unification, liberation or obliteration, a positive value or the expiration of all possibilities?

What attitude should we adopt *vis-a-vis* death? Defiance or submission, despair or expectation? Has the Christian religion enhanced or diminished the fear of it? In fact, why fear it if it is part of life like the horizon is part of the scenery? Is the fear of death justified? Can it be overcome? Is death, as Jung sees it, the fulfillment of life's meaning, the goal of life in its truest sense? Or is it the ultimate absurdity as proclaimed by Sartre? Does the East have an answer to the mystery? Is the traditional Christian approach valid for our day? But whatever death may be, mystery or problem, necessarily rooted in the nature of man, or unnatural, the enemy of mankind and the result of transgression, the first step is certainly to seek to define it.

II
DEFINITIONS

Traditionally a person is considered dead when breathing stops and the heartbeat ceases; but modern sophisticated methods make it possible to maintain "life" almost indefinitely, although the patient may never regain consciousness. The above definition is inadequate, however, because the heart can sometimes be revived. It is questionable whether a beating heart *per se* is a sign of "life."

Some physicians have argued that the existence of a living human brain should be the criterion of human life, the absence of brainwaves being the determining factor. Brainwaves can now be detected around the eighth week of pregnancy. If the brainwaves are flat, as measured by an electroencephalograph, the person may be considered dead, even if the heartbeat and breathing can be sustained with the help of special medical devices. At this point brain damage is irreversible and conscious life has ended. "The soul may already have left the body" stated Pope Pius XII in his address, "The Prolongation of Life." Bernard Ramm concurs, though in different terminology, when he writes, "If a man is no longer addressable as a person or a thou, if he no longer possesses the *humanum* or the *imago,* he is, from the standpoint of Christian theology, dead as a person." [1] Vital brain matter has been damaged and the possibility of regaining consciousness has disappeared.

Somatic death — when all vital functions have ceased — is gradually followed by cellular death. The cells in the body will continue to live for some time and muscles will respond to electrical stimulation.

In the absence of a universally acceptable definition of death

4

many ethical problems face the physician. What is his role? To relieve suffering or to prolong life artificially? Is such a life still meaningful? Are extraordinary means, regardless of the cost involved, really in the interest of the patient? Do they prolong suffering rather than life? Can a dying patient choose not to be treated? Can anyone else make this decision on behalf of the patient? When should extraordinary means be withdrawn with death to follow? When, if ever, and under what circumstances is it right to transplant tissues and organs of a hopelessly unconscious patient? Obviously it is incumbent upon the physician to take all reasonable, ordinary means of restoring the spontaneous vital functions and consciousness and if necessary to employ such extraordinary means as are available to him, but it cannot be obligatory to continue using extraordinary means indefinitely in hopeless cases.

It may be useful in passing to distinguish incurability from hopelessness. Diabetes, emphysema, and for that matter baldness and flat feet, are incurable but seldom hopeless. Even many types of cancer can be cured. So-called incurable patients have been known to live for considerable periods in cases where the disease lies dormant. In some instances there have been spontaneous cures.

When questioned regarding the use of modern techniques of artificial respiration in hopelessly unconscious patients, Pope Pius XII commented, "Since these forms of treatment go beyond the ordinary means to which one is bound, it cannot be held that there is an obligation to use them." [2] In fact, the State of Kansas has enacted a statute including a definition of death as "the absence of spontaneous brain function." At this point human life has ceased, regardless of the relative health of certain vital organs. Relationships with this world have been severed.

The idea of relationship is important. Life can be described as that force in an organism which places all other forces working in it in a serviceable relation to its growth and preservation. Life is the unifying factor that leads all the working forces in our body to seek a common goal — the building up of the body. Unity and life are related; without unity dissolution occurs. Death, by contrast, is a severance of relationships. On the physical level death is the violent separation of body and soul; on the spiritual level true life is found in union with God, in a relationship with him. When a man breaks away from God who is the fountain of life, the result is spiritual death. (Even on the social level, isolation and loneliness are foretastes of spiritual death). Eternal death consists in eternal separation from God, a total and permanent severance of all relationship with God and life.

Much about death remains mysterious. What is its cause? If the simple starfish can regrow missing parts and the salamander regenerate much of his missing body, why cannot the higher animals — especially man — do the same? Only skin and bone regrowth comes even close to a regenerative process. The lifetime of a cell or cell tissues varies considerably. Some cells die in ten or fourteen days; others are renewed over a period of ten years. When I meet someone after an interval of ten years I can be virtually certain that all the cells of his body are different from those I "saw" ten years previously, although I recognize the person without difficulty. The body is constantly deteriorating and renewing.

One might even speak of a potential immortality of the cellular elements of the body. The experiments of Dr. Alexis Carrel indicate that somatic cells do not have to die. Some animal tissues have been preserved outside the living organism for a time far exceeding the life-span of the organism from which they were taken. According to Dr. Carrel, "The removal of waste products and proper food prevent the occurrence of death. . . . the cells that build up the body are capable of unlimited multiplication. They are potentially immortal."[3]

To answer that death is merely a result of physiological de-

terioration is insufficient; theories about aging are tentative and uncertain. It has been suggested that aging and ultimately death may result from
- the progressive failure of cells to multiply efficiently in order to replace the normal, steady loss;
- the failure of an enzyme system;
- the accumulated damage from toxic substances which collect in the body;
- the accumulated effect of radiation to which we are inevitably exposed;
- the failure of the body to replace certain specialized cells when they are dead;
- the deterioration of cellular materials or of the surrounding matrix.

Life expectancy has risen considerably over the centuries, but this is small comfort in the face of ultimate death. The average Roman citizen lived only twenty-two years. In the Middle Ages the life span rose to thirty-five and improved very little throughout the eighteenth century. By 1840 the average life span reached forty-one in Great Britain, and by 1910 the U.S. registered fifty-two for men and fifty-five for women. In 1945 the mean was almost sixty-six and continues to rise slowly.

At the same time, the experience of death is less painful than is commonly assumed. The vast majority of terminal patients do not die in full consciousness; although the supposed agony may be fearful to watch, the patient is seldom conscious and the "agony" is not necessarily an indication of extreme pain. Of course few people ever witness an actual death since most dying persons are carefully segregated from the living and die in solitude. At least 80 percent of the U.S. population dies in intitutions — hospitals, nursing homes, or similar establishments. This is one of the most distressing aspects of dying. There is certainly no valid reason for the patient not to die at home, surrounded by loved ones who make the transition from life to death much easier.

But regardless of medical and psychological theories about aging and death, the mystery remains: why death?

The Bible furnishes an unequivocal answer: <u>Death is the result of sin</u> (Rom. 5:12). It is not a natural process. Man disregarded God, went his own way, failed to maintain his relationship with God, and the ensuing barrier between them resulted in man's death. The death threatened in Genesis 2:17, "In the day that you eat of it (i.e., the tree of knowledge of good and evil) you shall die," involved physical, spiritual, and eternal consequences.

Prior to the fall Adam's body was not subject to death, but this condition was subject to change. His condition was mutable and relative; the potential immortality of his body might be lost. The possibility became an actuality through disobedience. He heard the words, "You are dust and to dust you shall return" (Gen. 3:19).

But far more than physical death resulted from the fall. The death which had been threatened by God was the opposite of the life which had been promised and which included everything necessary for man's happiness. "As one man's trespass (Adam's) led to condemnation for all men, so one man's act of righteousness (Christ's) leads to acquittal and life for all men" (Rom. 5:18). Redemption through the death of Christ delivers from the curse of death which followed Adam's disobedience. Obviously, the main purpose of the death of Christ was salvation from spiritual and eternal death; but even as the threat of death embraced the totality of man's being — his physical, spiritual, and eternal attributes — so the redemption concerns the whole man as well.

Since the fall of man and the entrance of sin into the world, death has spread to all men. Sin and death belong together (Rom. 6:23), but the death of Christ has cancelled them both. Paradoxically, life grew out of the death of Christ; death is overcome in his resurrection and already its sting is removed from the believer. Christ's victory is a guarantee of our ultimate victory as well.

The Bible is careful not to attribute an inherent nobility to man's soul which would somehow result in immortality and eternal glory apart from the grace of God. Man lives under condemnation and wrath. Only Christ's redeeming death and triumphant resurrection can give hope and assurance to those who place their trust in the Redeemer. The Christian, freed from fear, can now live to serve the Lord (Rom. 14:7-9). Indeed, the believer has already passed from death to life; he has appropriated the death of Christ, died with Christ, and is no longer enslaved to sin as a controlling principle, but is alive to God. Accepting the death of Christ results in a new way of life. The Christian yields to God as one brought from death to life. Set free from the law of sin and death, the believer's life is based on a new principle — response to God's love as manifested in Jesus Christ, resulting in service to God and men.

Physical death had been a possibility in man's nature which ought to be removed through the tree of life but which instead became inevitable because of sin. But if physical death was not a necessity from the very beginning, if it had not occurred without man's transgression, would not the earth by now have been hopelessly over-populated? Of course there is no reason why God might not have interrupted natural procreation once the goal of filling the earth had been reached (Gen. 1:28). As soon as the earth had been full enough of living creatures this phase might have come to an end. Besides, there is no reason to assume that all the offspring of an increasing population should always remain on earth in an unchanged condition. Perhaps a transformation would have occurred similar to the change which will one day take place with the advent of the Lord, when the living shall be changed in the twinkling of an eye and the mortal put on immortality (I Cor. 15:51 ff.). Only speculative answers can be given to such theories.

Similarly, it is important to remember that death is not only at work among men; it reigns supreme in the animal and vegetable kingdom and did so quite obviously long before man came upon the scene. Can prehistoric death be the result of man's sin? An answer has been suggested that "death by sin" applies only to man, and that, in fact, the scientific principle that death is a necessary step in the organic process is distinctly affirmed in the New Testament (John 12:24; I Cor. 15:36 and cf. I Cor. 15:47a). There may be several other answers. For example, Scripture indicates that Satan is, in a special sense, the "prince of this world," and it may be that this earth was originally the special domain of Satan. Through his fall he may have brought death to the earth even as Adam's transgression brought death to mankind. Man was placed by God in a privileged position — Eden, a center of life — with the mandate to change the entire earth into a paradise. It is beyond the scope of this book to pursue these speculations, but they are intriguing and provide tentative answers to the riddle of death in prehistoric times.

III
EVASIONS

In *The Death of Ivan Ilych,* Tolstoy gives a masterful description of a man whose entire life had been one continuous evasion of the thought of death. Ivan Ilych had enjoyed a successful career. From governor's attaché he gradually rose to examining magistrate, became assistant prosecutor, and finally reached a yet higher position. Ivan's success was largely a result of his always being decorous, always doing the right thing (i.e. things approved by society). "Decorous" is a key word throughout the narrative.

His final promotion allowed Ivan to fulfill his dream of buying and furnishing an elegant home, free from vulgarity. He purchased antiques to give the place an aristocratic character. Furnishing the house became of such importance that Ivan became involved in the actual work; at one point he demonstrated how the curtains should be hung, mounted a stepladder, made a false step and slipped, knocking his side against the knob of the window frame. This created a pain which ultimately led to death.

It was this "false step" at the height of his career which led Ivan into reality. As of this moment life was no longer easy, pleasant, and decorous, composed of official relations with people on official grounds. His discomfort increased and gradually became alarming. Even his favorite pleasure, a card game similar to bridge, lost all attraction. Ivan was left with the awareness that his entire existence was poisoned. Conscious that he was dying he yielded to despair. He remembered a syllogism learned in logic: Caius is a man. Men are mortal. Therefore Caius is mortal. An abyss separated the theoretical concept from his personal experience; somehow he had never applied the syllogism to himself. Death had always remained an abstraction, a concept remote from personal preoccupations. Ivan could not even admit to himself that he was dying. "It can't be true. He would go to his study, lie down, and again be alone with It: face to face with It. And nothing could be done with It except to look at It and shudder." Still, the illusion and the deception continued. Even his family claimed that Ivan was the victim of a disease which could be cured.

Finally, in solitude toward the end of his life, Ivan hears "the voice of his soul" asking, "What is it you want?" The answer seems obvious: To live and not to suffer. But to the further question, "To live? How?" Ivan has no immediate answer. In reviewing his life he becomes aware of its trivial and superficial character, although — or because — he had done everything so properly.

Ultimately Ivan knows that he must die, and this awareness allows him to face death more realistically. Evasions are abandoned, illusions destroyed, hopes gone. From that moment on Ivan feels free to scream without reserve. His death becomes the moment of illumination and compassion, of concern for his family — and the fear of death disappears.

Consciously or unconsciously most people practice a form of evasion. The topic of death is seldom touched in conversation, and our funeral customs are a grotesque illustration of our perpetual evasions. Long before Tolstoy, the French philosopher Pascal wrote: "As men are not able to fight against death, misery, ignorance, they have taken it into their heads, in order to be happy, not to think of them at all" (*Pensées*, 168). He concluded that people seek constant diversion because "the natural poverty of our feeble and mortal condition [is] so miserable that nothing can comfort us when we think of it closely" (Ibid., 139). Man's restlessness results from his unwillingness to face his own condition. A ceaseless round of activities is "all that men have been able to discover to make themselves happy" (Ibid.). It is pointless to avoid the issue which must surely be confronted. Nevertheless, evasion or denial is apparently the first reaction of terminal patients.

The situation has not changed since Pascal wrote, and Ivan Ilych is still representative of most people. Evasions take different forms, but they are maintained. According to John Hinton, "There is no reason why the dying should not have the comfort of make-believe and even invite those around them to share these consoling day-dreams and not shatter them. At times they can again show full insight or give a hint to companions that they are well aware that this is a game, an acceptable facade. The convention of not talking directly about dying can often be a useful comfort to fall back upon." [1]

Often evasion takes refuge in philosophy. In *Overcoming the Fear of Death*, David Cole Gordon states forcefully that we should not repress the thought of death. "Insofar as we live with a fundamental belief which is untrue, is not much of our life converted into a lie?" He suggests that learning to live with the thought of finitude might work a powerful transformation in all our relationships and in our own lives. But the author defines death as an experience of unification, as part of an eternal cycle of merging with others and all. "It is the ultimate and final experience of unity, in which the body itself disintegrates and returns to the earth." Gordon concludes that this unity is the experience man seeks most avidly during his lifetime; in fact, it should be welcomed and desired. "Death, which has frightened man since his emergence as a thinking creature, is his ultimate and eternal unification experience. Death comes to all, not as a scourge or punishment, but as the culmination and fulfillment of life." [2] The unification envisioned here is not a life of eternal fellowship in the presence of God, but a merging with others and "all" in death, the return to dust. Is this really the supreme aspiration of man and can such a prospect eliminate the fear of death? Are we not victims of another evasion by embracing this viewpoint?

There are other evasive philosophic approaches. Wittgenstein

insisted that "death is not an event of life. Death is not lived
through." This is almost an echo of Goethe's thought that
death was no concern of his. For some bizarre reason Goethe
felt that his brilliant activity entitled him to immortality. "If
I work indefatigably until my end, then nature is obliged to
offer me another form of existence when the present one can
no longer endure my spirit." Elsewhere he remarks that "an
able human being who wants to amount to something over here
already, and therefore has to strive, to fight and to work daily,
leaves the world to come to take care of itself and is active and
useful in this one." It is quite true that we should make the
most of the gift of life, but it will hardly do to repeat with
Faust:

> Of the beyond I have no thought:
> When you reduce this world to naught,
> The other one may have its turn.
> My joys come from this earth, and there,
> That sun has burned on my despair:
> Once I have left those, I don't care:
> What happens is of no concern.[3]

Regardless of the "plague," we live as if we were immune. Life
must be "decorous" and every *faux pas* carefully avoided. The
very mention of death is socially unacceptable. The entire
process of death and dying is carefully secluded from the
daily experience of life. Some people cherish a nebulous pantheism; others have a vague sense of survival in and through
the human race. They should remember the words of John
Donne, "Any man's death diminishes me, because I am involved in Mankind; and therefore never send to know for
whom the bell tolls; it tolls for thee."

Many live with seeming unconcern, but are possessed by
the hyperactivism characteristic of Western man in general
and of the average American in particular. Evasions abound,
illusions are maintained, and death is seldom faced realistically.

IV

THE FEAR OF DEATH

Nietzsche labeled the fear of death a "European disease" and attributed it largely to the influence of Christianity. This accusation has been echoed ever since. According to David Cole Gordon, the dark feelings of fear, far from being diminished by any of the world's religions, are enhanced by them, particularly by Christianity because of its alleged premise that only the life hereafter really counts.[1] But the frequent argument that belief in an afterlife necessarily hampers the progress of mankind is devoid of historic evidence. It is enough to point to Christian activity and vitality throughout the centuries to show that this line of reasoning is defective. Similarly, it has sometimes been asserted that the fear of death is what produces the belief in an afterlife. Actually those who are dissatisfied with life often crave death, hoping for total extinction. Could it not also be said that the supposed finality of death is wishful thinking, an unwillingness to face the possibility of an afterlife?

At any rate the fear of death is universal and clearly antedates the Christian religion. It is found in the most primitive cultures around the world as well as in the most advanced. Indians to the west of Paraguay used to plant arrows around a sick man to keep death away; other tribes tried to catch the demon of death by means of hooks suspended from roofs and trees. In the ancient Babylonian *Epic of Gilgamesh*, the hero laments the death of his friend Enkidu: "Now what sleep is this that has taken hold of thee? Thou hast become dark and canst not hear me. When I die shall I be like Enkidu?

15

Sorrow entered my heart, I am afraid of death." La Roche-
foucauld (1613-1680) observed that "neither the sun nor
death can be looked at with a steady eye."

Long before the appearance of Christianity, the Greek poet
Sappho declared death to be the greatest of all evils. The gods
must think so too, she said, or else they would die.

> Sweet, passing sweet is light for men to see,
> Death is but nothingness!
> Who prays to die is mad.
> Ill life o'erpasseth glorious death.
> (Euripides, *Iphigeneia in Aulis* V. 1250ff.)

"Say not a word in death's favor," says Achilles. "I would
rather be a paid servant in a poor man's house and be above
ground, than a king of kings among the dead" (*Odyssey* XI,
488).

One could easily multiply quotations from dramatists and
philosophers of all cultures, past and present, to show that the
fear of death is universal. Death has always been considered
the supreme punishment one can inflict upon an enemy. It is
the supreme form of vengeance.

But the question remains why this universal fear exists. It
is particularly strong in North America, perhaps attributable in
part to the remarkable vitality of the population. Another,
more common reason perhaps is that many people seem to
believe that some sort of judgment follows death. The fact that
death is feared is obvious; the topic is excluded as carefully
from conversation as the subject of sex was in Victorian society.
People no longer die, they expire; undertakers are called
funeral directors, coffins are caskets, hearses are labelled coaches
or, better yet, professional cars; corpses are loved ones. There
are countless other euphemisms. People seem almost afraid to
call the thing by name lest they provoke it. The art of restoration permits the corpse to be seen in the semblance of normality.

Since outright denial is hardly feasible (except perhaps for
adherents of Christian Science), evasion is practiced on a broad

scale. It is an ancient art but hardly masks the deep-seated fears. Somehow we would like to believe with Epicurus that death does not concern us; that so long as we are alive death is not with us, and when death occurs we no longer exist.

But this is precisely the nagging question. If the biblical God exists, judgment after death is certain. If God does not exist death is annihilation and life becomes meaningless. Either way, fear seems to be the normal response. This is certainly the practical, down to earth situation.

Philosophers may decide that the fear of death is attributable to the abyss which separates time and eternity. Others may claim that man is afraid of death because of its mystery, its finality or uniqueness, or because of social, religious, or psychological conditioning, the uncertainty of the moment coupled with the certainty of the event — and the explanations abound. Do we really fear death because we are reduced to nothingness? Is total destruction so frightful? Or is it rather the possibility of survival that creates the fear? Is death feared because we die alone? In the deepest sense, is all fear ultimately the fear of death?

Tertullian discusses the question of fear in *The Soul's Testimony* (chapt. 4).

> Why dost thou fear death at all? There is nothing after death to be feared, if there is nothing to be felt. For though it may be said that death is distasteful . . . not for anything it threatens afterwards, but because it deprives of the good of life; yet, on the other hand, as it puts an end to life's discomforts, which are far more numerous, death's terrors are mitigated by a gain that more than outweighs the loss. And there is no occasion to be troubled about a loss of good things which is amply made up for so great a blessing as the relief from every trouble. There is nothing dreadful in that which delivers from all that is to be dreaded. If thou shrinkest from giving up life because thy experience of it has been sweet at any rate there is no need to be in an alarm about death if thou hast no knowledge that it is evil.
>
> The dread of it is the proof that thou art aware of its evil.

Thou wouldst never think it evil—thou wouldst have no fear of it at all—if thou were not sure that after it there is something to make it evil, and so a thing of terror.

Tertullian's reasoning is unimpeachable. His sentiments were echoed much later by Shakespeare in Hamlet's soliloquy.

>   To die: to sleep.
> To Sleep? perchance to dream. Ay, there's the rub;
> For in that sleep of death what dreams may come,
> When we have shuffled off this mortal coil,
> Must give us pause ....
> . . . the dread of something after death,
> The undiscovered country from whose bourn
> No traveller returns, puzzles the will,
> And makes us rather bear those ills we have
> Than fly to others that we know not of.
>   (*Hamlet* III, 1)

The fear of death is rooted in the fact that God must be faced — a thought which indeed inspires terror if we are not assured of acceptance and forgiveness. On the other hand, if God is denied, the sheer nothingness and emptiness of life deprives it of all meaning. At least Christianity took a realistic view of the situation and labeled death the enemy of man. Far from disparaging the gift of life because of the hereafter, the Christian can thoroughly enjoy life because he has been set free from the fear of death.

Of course, there are many other explanations for the widespread fear of death. It could be because man resists all change, and death is certainly the greatest change, by nature irrevocable. This theory would explain why older persons — more rigid and less inclined to change — are unwilling to face death, whereas young people are more open to discuss death and dying. Of course it is far from certain that young people are facing death more realistically. This kind of thing is hard to measure; and it may not be easy to establish a definite relationship between change and fear at all. Certainly all changes are not feared, only those which are injurious or uncertain. This would lead us back to the idea that the "unknown" is at the bottom of the fear of death.

If, as many advocate, death is simply a biological necessity conditioned by our finitude, why the resistance to it, the defiance, rage, and fear? If death is only natural, why such a widespread aversion? Obviously we cannot escape the human condition. Should we not then face the situation with courage and realism? Why indulge in repression and escapism? If death is simply a condition of finitude, why this irrational fear?

Another suggestion is that in death man is passive and helpless. But as a matter of fact, the same holds true for birth, and no one seems particularly anguished about being born. There is also another school of thought, which will be discussed in the next chapter, denying that man is passive at the moment of death.

As might well be expected, psychology has made its contribution to the topic. Freud postulated a death wish to explain this universal fear, calling it the strongest instinct in every living being and defining it as the desire to return to a previous state (i.e., the womb). In reality the strongest instinct is to live, and anything which appears to interfere with life is viewed as hostile and dangerous. If such an instinct existed it would help us to welcome death and hardly explain why it is feared. Besides, an instinct always moves toward the realization of its goal unless inhibited by obstacles or barriers (e.g., the sex drive). The death instinct would lead multitudes toward suicide.

To some extent the fear of death is healthy, for it serves to protect life and keeps us from assuming unnecessary risks. "The rational force of anxiety has perhaps been one of the strongest factors of progress in the struggle with nature, in the protection and enrichment of human life." [2]

Though philosophies and religions have endeavored to teach us to die well, few have taught us to die willingly. The terror of death remains regardless of medical and sociological progress or philosophic insight. The horror of it is universal among mankind, not so much because of the pain, but because of the mystery surrounding it. In our day the pain is significantly minimized. As we have already seen, few persons are conscious at the moment of death. An increasing drowsiness makes the terminal patient unaware of what is happening to him; the perception is clouded and full awakening seldom occurs. The natural progress of the disease and the use of drugs mean that for most patients the suffering is over before they actually die.

Some people claim total indifference in the face of death. David Hume insisted that "he was no more uneasy to think that he should not be after this life, than that he had not been before he began to exist"; to which Samuel Johnson remarked, "If he really thinks so, his perceptions are disturbed; he is mad: if he does not think so he lies. He may tell you, he holds his finger in the flame of a candle, without feeling pain; would you believe him? When he dies, he at least gives up all he has." To the question "Is the fear of death natural?" Johnson responded, "So much so, Sir, that the whole of life is but a keeping away of the thought of it."

Is it possible to come to terms with the problem of death? Is it a mystery which defies understanding? Can this fear be conquered? Does Christianity enhance or diminish it? If, as Montaigne believed, "to philosophize is to learn how to die," what contribution does philosophy make?

V

DEATH IN THE WESTERN TRADITION

Death has always puzzled man from the earliest ages. Primitive people were much closer to death in their day to day experience than most people are in our contemporary culture. Not only was the life-span much shorter, but people died surrounded by the family, the clan, or in some cases the tribe. Surprisingly enough, although it was common practice to observe death in primitive societies, it was never accepted as a purely natural event. Even in the most primitive cultures death was seen as an intrusion, an outside, hostile force coming into play, a mysterious power inflicting pain and punishment. It was assumed that the premature death of a man who was not injured or wounded indicated that he had become the victim of a sorcerer or of an evil spirit. Primitive man refused to rationalize death as fulfillment or as part of life even as the period is part of the sentence.

A brief overview of Greek and Roman thought is of particular interest to the Christian because the Gospel was first proclaimed in a world dominated by their ideas, and the sharp contrast between their speculations and the Gospel is most striking. On the other hand we should be aware of contemporary trends and will therefore later briefly examine the different attitudes regarding death prevalent in today's thinking.

To the early Greeks death was terrible, especially because the world seemed so beautiful and delightful. The inevitability of death cast a pall over all of life; its grim reality stood in sharp contrast to the intense desire to live and to the beauty of the universe.

Euripides declared that nothing is sweeter than to behold the

21

light of the sun, and regardless of the miseries of life, old age is no longer felt as a burden when death finally approaches. He complained that death carries away both young and old without discrimination. "Is it not my function to take the doomed?" asks Death at the beginning of *Alcestis*. "No," replies Apollo. "Only to dispatch those who have ripened into full old age." In other words, death may be acceptable at the end of a long life because it is "the course of Nature" and seems to be the law of the universe. Euripides advises us to face death with resignation, to endure because we must and not to chafe.

The Stoic philosophers taught that man should be indifferent to everything except virtue and vice. Sickness, pain, and death should simply be ignored. Religion was accepted as necessary for morality, and even superstitions were tolerated. In fact, Chaldean astrology was highly regarded by the Stoics because it assumed a certain harmony throughout the universe. Their theology was a compromise between pantheism and theism; the universe is a living being of which God is the soul, the sovereign law, the animating principle. The world constitutes the body of God. The human soul is composed of matter, but the decomposition of the body does not necessarily involve the destruction of the soul. Although there may not be a hereafter for all men, the soul of the sage — more vigorous than that of common mortals — survives. The sage is not affected by the events of either life or death. Let come what may, he is resigned, for everything is decreed by Nature and Fate. Stoicism was immensely popular among the intellectuals, but their lofty doctrines failed to reach the masses.

The Stoic philosopher Epictetus viewed death as "the time . . . for matter once again to dissolve into the elements out of which it was composed." Democritus has no better answer to the mystery of death than to proclaim the mortality of the soul, which, along with everything else, is composed of indivisible and unchangeable atoms which are dispersed at death. "When the dust has drained the blood of man, once he is slain, there is

no return to life," declares Aeschylus (*Eumenides*, 648).
Sophocles refers to man as a mere phantom, a fleeting shadow,
and affirms that "no man is so foolish that he is enamored
of death."

Plato made one of the most significant contributions to the
concept of death and immortality. Believing that man com-
bines both immortal and mortal elements, he deduces the immortality of the soul from its simplicity (which renders it
incorruptible), from the goodness of the Creator, and from its
being the very principle of life. Plato assumed that transition
from being to nonbeing was impossible, adding that the very
desire of the philosopher to be free from the fetters of the body
and his wish to commune with the intelligible world demon-
strates the immortality of the soul.

Intelligence considers matter as its natural enemy, as the
seat and source of evil. The mind longs to be freed from the
body because the visible world is a prison, a place of correc-
tion. The Christian concept of resurrection would have horri-
fied Plato, for he saw death as a release of the soul from the
body; but his speculative thought has influenced Christian
thinking in spite of its non-Christian concepts (such as the
eternity of matter and the pre-existence of the soul). Many
Christians seem to have the unbiblical notion that to be removed from matter is to be close to God. The Bible always sees
man as a total unit, body and soul, flesh and spirit. The body
and the soul are not two completely distinct components re-
luctantly held together until the soul is finally liberated from
the prison of the body at death. In fact, the soul without the
body is "naked" (2 Cor. 5:1-4). It is only when man's soul
is united with his resurrected body that he enters fully into
bliss.

Aristotle believed in the eternity of matter but rejected the
distinction between form and matter advocated by Plato. According to Aristotle, the Idea of a thing cannot exist apart from
the thing itself; it is inherent in the thing. The logical conse-
quence is a firm denial of individual immortality.

Epicurus offered a different solution to the riddle of existence, maintaining that reason must avoid pointless speculation and confine itself to the experiences of the senses. Mind and soul are merely other forms of matter which die with the body. If death were the transition to a higher life, reasons Epicurus, man would rejoice in its coming. On the other hand, the fear of death is not caused by the dread of non-existence; we fear death because we mistakenly associate feeling with a future state of nothingness, as if we could feel the void and emptiness of eternity. In reality we should believe that "death is not an evil; neither for him who is dead, for he has no feeling; nor for the living, for him death does not yet exist. As long as we are alive, death does not exist for us, and when death appears we no longer exist."

Of course the fatal flaw of this argument is obvious, for it is precisely the very fact that we shall cease to exist which troubles us most. The presupposition that death ends everything is easy to make but impossible to demonstrate. Unfortunately, as we have already pointed out, death penetrates all of life, and it is hardly correct to say that the living can simply ignore it.

Seneca, a contemporary of Paul, suggested that it is possible to overcome the fear of death by thinking about it constantly. Since life inevitably moves toward death, why fear it? Charlemagne prepared for death by contemplating skulls, listening to funeral music, dressing in funeral attire, and even sleeping in his coffin. Such an intense preoccupation would appear only to enhance the fear. Montaigne realized that to live in a constant state of preparedness enslaves one to the thought of death, concluding that "we trouble life by our concern with death, and we trouble death by our concern with life."

The problem of death and immortality was discussed with renewed seriousness in the eighteenth century. Total annihilation (as had been proclaimed by the Stoics) was advocated by French materialists and opposed by Kant. The Romantics by contrast upheld a strange glorification of death. Subsequently the pendulum has swung back and forth from sanguine optimism to extreme pessimism. Today philosophers are torn between the possibility of non-being and the terror and burden of being.

Heidegger (1889-   ) has exerted considerable influence on modern Western thought, although relatively few people have first-hand knowledge of his writings. Heidegger tries to find a clue to the meaning of life in the fact of death. For him death occupies a key position in the investigation of Being.

Heidegger is not primarily concerned with the origin of death or life after death, but with the significance of death as an intrinsic part of human experience, as part of man's essential being. Existence can be defined as a "being-towards-death," death being at the core of existence, hovering over us and dominating us from the moment of birth.

How can death be investigated? It is impossible to become involved and to record the experience. One cannot experience death and then philosophize or analyze. In contrast to the suggestion that the death of others can be observed and furnish sufficient clues, Heidegger would insist that death is specifically mine, that no one can experience it for me. He thus concludes that

— Death is always my most personal experience, totally my own;
— Death is non-relational. In death all relationships are dissolved; I die alone;
— Death is unsurpassable; it cannot be outstripped, representing the most extreme possibility.

By "possibility" Heidegger does not mean something that may happen in the future. A "possibility" is a way of being and acting which is open to me now as I face a specific situation. In all my decisions I must be aware of death as a possibility, and it is in the light of death that all other possibilities must be evaluated. It is precisely this threefold awareness which gives authenticity to life. The thought of death is not evaded — is never evaded. It is used to create authenticity.

Death is a mode of being because as soon as we are born we are old enough to die. All of life is lived in the presence of death. This authentic human existence results in anxiety; there are no illusions. Human existence is characterized by death and will have to come face to face with Nothingness. Man comes from nothing, is nothing, and moves toward nothingness.

Heidegger goes a step further. Aware that all of being is permeated by death and moves toward death, I resolutely take death upon myself, accept it as part of my human condition. I anticipate death, claim it as my own, and thereby gain freedom for death.

If the very structure of existence is a "being-towards-death" it is not surprising that "authenticity" generates anxiety. Yet, at the same time, Heidegger claims that such a realistic viewpoint sets man free. The awareness that all my existence is only a "being-towards-death" helps me to rise above the petty, trivial daily vexations and the many small incidents which constitute daily life. At the same time, since death is uniquely my own and I must die alone, my individuality is reaffirmed. I can no longer take refuge in anonymity or be part of the crowd. Life becomes authentic, real.

Heidegger does not furnish an answer to the problem of death. Instead he challenges us to live authentically, to avoid all evasions, to be conscious of our finitude, of the nature of our being. He admonishes us to allow anxiety to lead us to relentless confrontation with the fact that our whole being is towards death. Since any comfort would only result in an inauthentic mode of being, all hope is negated. Man is admonished to accept the inevitable, or better yet, to anticipate death and to use the knowledge gained to live authentically. This resolute acceptance of death yields freedom — freedom for death. But is such a detached attitude really possible? Is it within the psychological power of man to be intellectually and emotionally detached in the face of death — in the face of MY death — especially a death which leads to nothingness? Does it really help to make decisions always conscious of the possibility of death? Instead of authenticity such an attitude could easily produce paralysis. Each and every choice becomes deadly serious, each decision one of life and death. The sole result may well be an inability to decide in the light of eternal darkness and nothingness.

Sartre (1905-   ) would take sharp issue with Heidegger. Far from seeing death as a possibility in the sense that we have various choices of being and acting which are open to us, Sartre would say that death is the cancellation of all possibilities and therefore the ultimate absurdity. Sartre would agree with Heidegger that we should constantly be prepared for death, but he admits that the theory is easier than the practice. No matter how much we take death into account, it is often unexpected. Intelligent plans can be formulated while still recognizing that we are finite and must die, but how can we be sure to die in old age? On the other hand it is impossible to plan for a premature death. Such an attitude would eliminate all plans and goals since premature death is unexpected and can happen at any moment. We are like a man condemned to death who is bravely preparing himself for the ultimate penalty and who is meanwhile carried off by the flu. Since I cannot forsee the date of MY death, concludes Sartre, I cannot wait for it.

Since death is not rooted in freedom it can only deprive life of all meaning. If the "closing of the account" is not free, it matters little whether all the other decisions of life have been free. After all, the "closing of the account" gives life its meaning and its value. Sartre recalls an anecdote of Diderot about two brothers who appeared before the divine tribunal. The first said to God, "Why did you make me die so young?" And God said, "In order to save you. If you had lived longer, you would have committed a crime as your brother did." Then the second brother in turn asked, "Why did you make me die so old?" Since the moment of death is not freely chosen, reasons Sartre, freedom is an illusion. Death can never give meaning to life; it destroys all projects, cancels everything. Death cannot be precisely predicted; it disarms expectations and reaches us from the outside. At the moment of death the past becomes "fixed," petrified, solidified. The meaning of a particular life is thus "fixed." My contemporaries now become the guardians of my past and determine the attitude of others towards it. They may even forget me, and this too is an attitude.

Regardless of his pessimistic outlook, Sartre claims that death frees us. In revealing itself to us as it really is, death liberates us from its alleged constraint. Sartre's definition of freedom is simply an "autonomy of choice," be it an intention or action. Of course, man can choose to die; a voluntary death is always a possibility, but this can hardly be called "freedom" in the commonly accepted sense of the word, since man cannot choose not to die. Generally speaking, freedom is defined as the ability to choose and to reach certain goals. But for Sartre success is not related to freedom. It is not necessary to obtain what we want in order to be free. It is enough to be autonomous. According to Sartre, man can assert his liberty by inflicting death upon himself. He can reject the burden of existence, escape the nausea which is attached to being.

Sartre would say that death does not concern us, that it does not penetrate us because it does not belong to us. Only the future gives meaning to our actions, but death has no future and it is therefore not an authentic human act. For this very reason death does not reach me. I am free; I escape death, although the thought of it may well haunt me.

Sartre insists that man can and should die with dignity and integrity. Unfortunately, the concept of integrity remains undefined. In one of Sartre's stories, *The Wall,* the main character, Pablo, is condemned to be shot. Waiting for his execution, Pablo realizes that he had never thought of death up to this point, but now he has nothing else to do. Not wishing to "die like a beast," he longs to understand. His life appears to him as shut up, closed like a bag, although the content is as yet incomplete (death is always unexpected). Pablo decides to die properly, but the author fails to define a proper death. Pablo could have saved his own skin by betraying a comrade, but refuses, for no particular reason, perhaps simply for the sake of obstinacy. Values such as comradeship or political convictions do not come into play. In fact, patriotism, friendship, love, "death had disenchanted everything. Life had no value, all meaning is lost."

Sartre concludes that death simply cannot be interpreted as part of life. Existence is not a "being-towards-death." If death could be called the final chord of a melody then we must also remember that the final chord looks toward the silence, towards "the nothingness of sound which follows the melody." The silence which inevitably follows is already present in the last chord "as its meaning." Death is totally absurd and every attempt to consider it as a resolved chord at the end of a melody must be sternly rejected. Death is not part of life; it comes to us from the outside and transforms us into the outside. Death removes all meaning from life.

Jaspers (1883-1969) enlarges upon an earlier thought, that "if to philosophize is to learn how to die, then this learning how to die is actually the condition for the good life. To learn to live and to learn to die are one and the same thing."

If Sartre finds existence an "unbearable weight," Jaspers on the other hand speaks of the "fragility of being." He sees death as an "ultimate situation" along with guilt and the uncertainties of the world. According to Jaspers, such ultimate situations bring us face to face with the reality of failure. The next question is what to do in the face of absolute failure. Jaspers rejects the advice of the Stoics. "To withdraw to our own freedom in the independence of the mind is not adequate. The Stoic's perception of man's weakness was not radical enough. . . . The Stoic leaves us without consolation; the independent mind is barren, lacking all content" because the mind depends on what is put into it from the outside. The Stoic doctrine, says Jaspers, affords no opportunity of inner transformation. Yet, "the way in which man approaches his failure determines what he will become." Our response to the "failure" which we face because of death is crucial.

Not only the Stoic answer to the problem of death, but all answers must be resolutely rejected. It is essential for man to reach the point of total despair. We must face the unalterable situation and recognize it for what it is. "In ultimate situations man either perceives nothingness or senses true being." Jaspers will opt for true being.

The Christian concept of immortality (or more correctly, eternal life) is rejected. Jaspers repeats with Lessing that immortality in the sense of a future existence would be infinitely dull. Besides, if I am assured of my place in heaven I grow more indifferent to the world.

Jaspers summarizes the basic human situation as an existence in the world without knowing whence or whither. When man faces death, when he faces an ultimate situation where he reaches a boundary, a limit, he can either opt for nothingness or authentic being. To choose nothingness would lead to despair, and "even despair, by the very fact that it is possible in the world, points beyond the world." Our hopes and aspirations guarantee the possibility of fulfillment.

The intense anxiety experienced in an ultimate situation becomes the redeeming force, the turning point toward transcendence. Fear must turn into a power "that compels men to save themselves in the sphere of reason; then it can evoke the will that grasps its meaning before Transcendence, transforms man, and makes him true. The great fear of mankind can be a creative fear, and then it will work like a catalyst for the emergence of freedom."

This elevation into Transcendence defies explanation. Man enters into the "encompassing," the embracing or the enveloping, a sort of "cosmic weather," an all-pervading atmosphere in which particular things are bathed and which, nevertheless, transcends them all. The "Encompassing" can be called "God" and is totally unimaginable.

To summarize, Jaspers demands a serious awareness of death

as an ultimate situation; in the face of death all evasions must be avoided and all comfort be rejected. One must choose freely to flounder, to suffer shipwreck in order to gain authenticity. Through this action transcendence, an entrance into the encompassing, is attained; true being is realized, and this transcendence transforms man into God.

Camus' (1913-1960) attitude toward death is graphically depicted in his novel *The Plague*. An entire city, Oran, is victimized by the plague. Throughout the novel the plague is a transparent symbol of death.

Camus describes the reactions of different people facing certain death. At first the newspapers play down the plague, and City Hall refuses to acknowledge the gravity of the situation for fear of creating a panic. At first the inhabitants of Oran "went on doing business, arranged for journeys, and formed views. How should they have given thought to anything like a plague, which rules out any future, cancels journeys, silences the exchanges of views. They fancied themselves free, and no one will ever be free as long as there are pestilences."

Although the plague made deep inroads, the "townsfolk apparently found it hard to believe what was happening to them. . . . Nobody as yet had really acknowledged what the disease connoted." Of course people were worried and irritated, but these are not feelings with which to confront the plague.

Father Paneloux delivers a sermon in the cathedral of Oran and startles his audience with his opening words, "Calamity has come upon you, my brethren, and, my brethren, you deserve it." To some "the sermon simply brought home the fact that they had been sentenced for an unknown crime to an indeterminate period of punishment." After Paneloux witnesses the painful agony of a child, he preaches once more. Privately he had admitted that the horrible death of a child "is revolting because it passes our human understanding"; but, he had added, "perhaps we should love what we cannot understand."

In his second sermon Paneloux confesses that death is beyond all rational explanations. "We" — and Paneloux was now saying "we" instead of "you" — we must believe that "all trials, however cruel, work together for good to the Christian. And, indeed, what a Christian should always seek in his hour of trial is to discern that good, in what it consists and how he can best turn it into account." Paneloux suggests that instead of explaining, the Christian must learn what the trial teaches, and concludes that in the final analysis, faced with the ultimate test, "we must believe everything or deny everything."

The chronicler of the events is Dr. Rieux, who pursues his duties and opposes the plague vigorously with every means at his disposal. Although all hope of victory is vain, a supreme effort must be made to win temporary inroads. Dr. Rieux muses that the order of the world is shaped by death, and so it might be better for God if we refused to believe in him. We shall simply continue to struggle against death with all our might without raising our eyes toward heaven where God sits in silence.

But Dr. Rieux was the exception. In general the people of Oran "had fallen into line, adapted themselves, as people say, to the situation, because there was no way of doing otherwise. Naturally they retained the attitudes of sadness and suffering, but they had ceased to feel their sting. Indeed to some, Dr. Rieux among them, this precisely was the most disheartening thing: that the habit of despair is worse than despair itself."

Tarrou joined Rieux in his efforts to defeat the plague, but he does not assume personal innocence and learns that throughout his life he had been infected with the plague. Finally the plague reaches Tarrou, who does not want to die. " 'I shall put up a fight. But, if I lose the match, I want to make a good end of it.' Rieux: 'No. To become a saint you need to live. So fight away.' " The refusal to accept death, the firm resolution to defy it, is ultimately all Camus can suggest in the face of the inevitable. Death is scandalous, an absurdity, and therefore unacceptable. The answers of Paneloux are insufficient. To trust without understanding is impossible. The fact that such an attitude of defiance is pointless and doomed, since death will conquer all resistance, only intensifies the vigorous opposition. One is reminded of the words of Dylan Thomas:

> Do not go gentle into that good night. . . .
> Rage, rage against the dying of the light.

VI
DEATH IN THE EASTERN TRADITION

Although the Eastern traditions regarding life and death differ enormously from those commonly held in the West, it may be well to examine some of the basic tenets held by the majority of Eastern thinkers. The very fact that their perception of ultimate reality is so vastly different should be of interest to us. Besides, the influence of Eastern thought has been growing throughout the West and deserves thoughtful consideration.

Hinduism tolerates a large variety of individual beliefs. Having no distinct creeds, it has been called an encyclopedia of all religions and appears to be a collection of many overlapping forms. Some Hindus are atheists, others pantheists (stressing the ultimate unity of all things), and others theists. But they all agree that life is only one long series of sufferings and that the aim of religion is to deliver man from pain. Most, if not all, Hindus would also agree that the doctrine of rebirth is central to all other teachings. As Dr. Suzuki explains it, transmigration "affords us the chance of pilgrimaging throughout the whole universe, from the thirty-three heavens to the nineteen hells," including many other realms. Admittedly, it "is not at all pleasant to be fighting all the time, to be tortured in various ways, or to be eternally hungry," but "it is in accord with human nature to experience vicissitudes of existence and thereby to learn to read the meaning of life." [1]

One of the strongest influences in Hinduism is the teaching of *Shankara,* who lived in the eighth century. According to Shankara, the world is nothing but illusion (*Maya*), and the only absolute reality is *Brahma.* There is no starting point, no beginning, and no end, only an infinite succession of creations and reabsorbtions into the One. All else is but mirage or dream. There is no individual immortality because the individual self is only an illusion along with everything else. The only Self is *Brahma*.

In opposition to Shankara, a religious order was formed by *Ramanuja* in the twelfth century. This thinker modified the absolute monism of Shankara, teaching that all is contained within God but at the same time allowing a certain plurality within the unity. Thus Ramanuja affirmed the reality of this world and maintained that the human soul is different from God and that it shall not be absorbed into *Brahma*. Souls are either eternally released or bound, and their ultimate fate is determined by knowledge. But true knowledge does not lead to the extinction of personality, as Shankara taught, but to the experience of bliss. After death, souls are connected with bodies in accordance with deeds done in life. But as well as through knowledge, man can also relate to God through devotion. A life of bliss in the presence of God in heaven is the solution to the problem of pain.

Different views were proclaimed by *Madhva* in the following century. Along with most other Hindu thinkers, he agreed that all is pain and pain alone, but he maintained a dualistic perspective. Madhva stressed the real distinction between God and the soul, God and matter, soul and matter, and emphasized the uniqueness of each human being. He taught eighteen means to achieve the right knowledge of God. Among them is the service of Vishnu, represented by branding the symbol of Vishnu on the body. According to Madhva, not only can man ultimately reach bliss in heaven, but eternal damnation in hell is a definite negative possibility as well. It would seem that Madhva was the only significant Hindu teacher who taught the possibility of eternal perdition (a possible influence of Christianity).

Buddhism has erected the disillusionment with life into a system. To be delivered from pain and suffering one must attain *nirvana*. Theoretically Buddhism denies the transmigration of the soul because the idea of a soul existing in the body is not part of Buddhist teaching. What lives on after death is not the soul, but *karma,* which is defined as the result of what has happened before. The true Buddhist holds to rebirth without transmigration. Everything in the universe is relative and impermanent, including the individual self.

> Misery only doth exist; none miserable.
> No doer is there; naught but the deed is found.
> Nirvana is, but not the man who seeks it.
> The path exists, but not the traveller on it.

Nirvana is not the liberation of the soul, but the replacement of an impermanent state by a permanent one. There is no individual existence in nirvana, but the experience of nirvana is nonetheless real.

The path to nirvana is through pure acts (i.e., acts free from desire, acts which do not contribute to existence and are by their nature destroyers of existence, thereby leading to nirvana). Active love and devotion to fellowmen is to be avoided as much as all other action prompted by desire, regardless of motivation. Buddhism is also hostile to work since this implies a clinging to things. Death is the obvious sign of the impermanence of all things, and it follows that meditation on the subject of death will lead to a clearer grasp of reality and is highly recommended. The place where the dead are burned is most suitable for meditation.

The original Buddhist doctrine has undergone many variations. There is a significant difference, for example, between Mahayana and Hinayana Buddhism, the latter claiming that nirvana can be achieved here and now through meditation; but meditation is a luxury reserved almost exclusively to monks. Mahayana Buddhism on the other hand stresses that nirvana can be reached in many different ways but takes centuries to achieve. Both laymen and monks can attain it through worship as well as through meditation. Proper rites erase evil.

This teaching gave birth to pompous ritual, rich liturgy, and the cult of Buddha.

Two of the most striking innovations of Mahayana Buddhism have been the introduction of a Supreme Reality from which the universe emanated, and the doctrine of individual immortality. The way to eternal bliss is faith in the Buddha and Boddhisattvas. The latter are persons who had nirvana within their grasp, rejected it, and voluntarily accepted additional rebirths in order to help other people attain salvation. The Boddhisattvas thereby accumulated a huge reservoir of merit which, in turn, could be transferred to those who would otherwise be unworthy of nirvana.

To this modification of the karma theory was added another concept called the *Pure Land School,* which characterizes almost all Chinese Buddhism and has exercised considerable influence in Japan. The idea is that a Pure Land created by Buddha Amitabha (or Amida as he is known in Japan) exists in the West; those who call upon Amida in faith will be translated to the Pure Land where conditions for final liberation are excellent. The Japanese Pure Land Sect (founded by Honen, A.D. 1133-1212) lays particular stress on the 18th of the 48 vows of Amida, reliance on which is essential. It reads: "If the beings of the ten quarters — when I have attained Enlightenment — blissfully trust in me with the most sincere mind, wish to be born in my country, and chant the name of Buddha ten times, but are not so born, may I never obtain the State of Enlightenment. Excluded, however, are those who have committed the Five Deadly Sins and who have abused the true *dharma.*"

It matters little whether the predisposition of the adherent is toward good or evil. The efficacy of the vow does not depend on the purity or impurity of the body, nor on time, place, or opportunity. Even sinners, as sinners, are eligible for rebirth in the Pure Land if they simply invoke the name of Amitabha, who vowed that he would not accept perfect bliss until he knew that all who invoked his name might be saved.

According to Honen, salvation is not attained through individual ascetic practices but through faith in Amitabha and reliance on his vow. Honen's admonition to "renounce, shut, ignore and throw away" is one of the most famous assertions in the history of Japanese Buddhism, meaning that one must "renounce" the reliance on self-discipline or asceticism, "shut" the gate of silent meditation, "ignore" all devices, and "throw away" all knowledge, only concentrating on invoking the Buddha.

As might well be expected, speculation arose on the intermediate state between death and rebirth. The terrors which are faced during this time are vividly portrayed, and advice is furnished on how rebirth in the most painful condition can be avoided.

In practice most Japanese are both Buddhists and Shintoists. The latter is of pure Japanese origin and is characterized by an ancestor worship similar to that practiced in China. The deceased person becomes a *kami,* or a supernatural being, and is worshipped on memorial days with prayers and sacrifices. Standing before the ancestor tablet (a simple board eight inches high, of white, unlacquered wood) the members of the family say, "I speak to you, exalted soul of our father, who has become a god." Out of 125 deceased monarchs only twelve emperors and three empresses are officially worshipped as gods. The influence of the dead is enormous; every day they must be thanked and worshipped to the point that they have become tyrants over the living.

Jainism, in common with Buddhism and Hinduism, holds to the impermanence of all things. Personal asceticism is relied upon for deliverence. The degree of self-mortification is extraordinary, and the ideal death of a saint is to perish through self-imposed, slow starvation. Jainism considers monasticism the ideal life. Transmigration and knowledge delivers the soul from the recurring cycle of birth and death. Those who have attained nirvana are worshipped, especially the twenty-four Tirthankaras, saints whose invocation helps the supplicant attain nirvana.

In China, ancestor worship is the oldest form of religion. Life after death is seen as a replica of life on earth; the emperor still rules, although after a few generations he passes into obscurity and is replaced by another deceased emperor.

Confucius, in common with other Chinese, believed in the survival of the soul after death; but in response to a question for additional clarification he simply stated, "While we do not know life, how can we know about death?" Actually, the teaching of Confucius was not religious but ethical and was based on the inherent goodness of man. In this system the reward of virtue is long life and the preservation of a good name after death.

When Confucianism was adopted as the state religion, the authorities established three sacrifices per year for the souls of the departed. Despite the agnosticism of Confucius, ancestor worship flourished under his system. Every house featured a small chapel in the southwestern corner. Communion with the dead could be established through sacrifice or divination. Ancestral tablets were kept in the home during periods of mourning and subsequently brought to the ancestral hall of the clan. By imperial edict sacrifices were offered to Confucius and temples erected in all major cities. The ancestor cult has been the dominant form of religion in China, and the invisible ancestors are always present in the minds of the Chinese.

Chinese speculation reached its climax in *Taoism*. The Taoist strives to live in harmony with Tao (the Way) and thus hopes to participate in the eternal order of things, thereby gaining a sort of immortality. Lao-Tse, the traditional founder of Taoism who may have lived during the sixth century, gives a detailed characterization of Tao:

> The Way is like an empty vessel
> That may yet be drawn from
> Without ever needing to be filled;
> It is bottomless . . .
> It is like a deep pool that never dries

> When you look at it you cannot see it;
> It is called formless.
> When you listen to it you cannot hear it;
> It is called soundless.
> When you try to seize it you cannot hold it;
> It is called subtle.
> No one can measure these three to their
>   ultimate ends,
> Therefore they are fused to one.

The Tao is difficult to define; it is formless and shapeless, has neither front nor back, but it is essential to hold on to the Way. It is an eternal, unchanging, all-pervading principle, totally inactive yet highly effective. The Tao acts spontaneously (not rationally) and it is essential for man to be in harmony with it. Therefore all virtue consists in the suppression of the self (freedom from desire) and of all but spontaneous action. Man must become free from all involvement and fall back into the ultimate ground or Tao. The ultimate goal is eternal emptiness, the absolute void, the fullness of nothingness.

Taoism and Zen Buddhism are parallel in their de-emphasis of reason and in their objectives, except that Zen Buddhism hopes to reach the goal through illumination. Thinking or logical reasoning will never clear up problems of religious significance, according to Zen Buddhism. The links with the mystical traditions of the West are obvious.

The ethereal philosophy of the great thinkers is far removed from the concerns of the masses, but a particularly strong objective of popular Taoism is longevity. This helps explain the popularity of the Pure Land Doctrine and the simple desire for long life, despite the strong tradition that life is illusion and pain. Since not everyone can become a monk, achieve total detachment and concentrated meditation, the loftiest teachings degenerate quickly into magic formulas, alchemy (the quest for the elixir of life), and breathing exercises. Thus Taoism becomes a mass of superstitions.

Not only was Taoism engulfed by these trends, but Buddhism

developed a rich mythology which captivated the imagination of the people and nourished their natural fear of death. Hinduism also developed elaborate ceremonies related to death, especially for the upper classes. After cremation the ashes are cast into a river, as are the bones which are gathered a few days later. Offerings are presented to the dead because the ghost needs nourishment to acquire a phantom-like body which will enable him to travel to the next existence. After ten days of ritual uncleanness everyone related to the dead may resume normal occupations. The idea that ceremonial uncleanness is associated with death (especially strong in the Old Testament) is well-nigh universal and might provide interesting clues to understanding the origin and nature of the concept of death.

In both East and West, regardless of the claims of philosopher or religious teacher to serenity in the face of death, the problem of dying is not solved on a practical, down-to-earth level, and the fear of death continues to poison daily existence.

VII
CHRISTIAN PERSPECTIVES

Given the variety of human experience, it would be surprising to find only one valid attitude toward death outlined in the Scriptures. Some may dogmatically insist that only one biblical attitude toward death is sound, but such a viewpoint is superficial. The dynamic and manifoldness of Christian experience reflects the wealth of biblical teaching on death. There are, of course, basic underlying principles running through all of Scripture. It is precisely when man faces death that he is reminded of the dignity bestowed upon him at creation when he was made in the image of God.

At one point the psalmist describes a man who trusts in his wealth and boasts of the abundance of his riches, but observes soberly that wealth is no guarantee against death. A rich man too will ultimately die. He "cannot abide in his pomp, he is like the beasts that perish" (Psalm 49:20). He who fails to discern true values and estimates wealth more than spiritual life and fellowship with God, lives and dies like a beast. This is abnormal because man differs qualitatively from animals. He is made in the image of God, called to reflect the person of God. Although the image has been marred and the likeness ruined, man is still human. He should not abase himself and move on the animal level. True, man is no longer at his best, but he is nevertheless man and not beyond redemption. Man is still the object of God's loving concern, therefore man's death has meaning — a God-given meaning. It is not merely a biological necessity shared with the animal world. The death of man does not only diminish the species by one. Each person is unique, irreplaceable, an individual with a special relationship to God, mankind, and the world, a being with responsibility and freedom. For such a creature to perish like a beast is tragic, a monstrosity, a denial of his true humanity. Such a death must be the culmination of a wasted life, exclusively concerned with material things.

The same point is driven home in the story of the rich fool whose life was only the total sum of his possessions (Luke 12:16-21). During his life appearances were in his favor, but in reality he stood under the shadow of divine judgment. His premature death was therefore the culmination of an empty life, devoid of authenticity. Apparently nothing could shake this man out of his false sense of security. He had successfully evaded the thought of death.

It is strange that we should have to be reminded of the transience of life, but the Bible stresses this idea over and over again lest we should forget our mortality.

> Lord, let me know my end,
> and what is the measure of my days;
> let me know how fleeting my life is;
> Behold, thou hast made my days a few handbreadths,
> and my lifetime is as nothing in thy sight.
> Surely every man stands as a mere breath!
> Surely man goes about as a shadow!
>
> (Psalm 39:4ff.)

Since life is constantly moving toward death, reminders of our mortality should not be necessary, but strangely enough we may well have to learn to pray with the psalmist, "Let me know how fleeting my life is." The danger of being totally absorbed in "things" is even greater in a relatively wealthy society where the dead and dying have become largely invisible. Even Moses prayed, "So teach us to number our days that we may get a heart of wisdom" (Psalm 90:12). To "get a heart of wisdom," to gain insight and self-knowledge, is directly related to our awareness of death (cf. James 4:13-17). The brevity of life should lead to reflection, to self-knowledge which is mediated through the knowledge of God. This attitude will keep us from dying "like the beasts that perish." Physical death has far more than biological significance; death is unique. Even as spiritual life is not merely enhanced natural vitality, but belongs to a totally different realm, even so my death is far more than a biological fact which I share with the rest of creation.

The normal instinct of self-preservation is not abolished in the Christian; with the rest of animate creation he abhors death and embraces life. Though he is not passive in death, the Christian accepts the divine decision. Even in the experience of death the believer remains in fellowship with Jesus Christ. In this connection a statement of Paul's is significant: "None of us lives to himself, and none of us dies to himself. If we live, we live to the Lord, and if we die, we die to the Lord, so then, whether we live or whether we die, we are the Lord's" (Rom. 14:7, 8). This is not an admonition to a godly life; Paul states a fact. Faith implies that one lives to God. This is a necessary corrollary of faith. He who has responded to God's call through Jesus Christ enters into a relationship of trust with God. Such an attitude becomes characteristic of life . . . and death. Even as the Christian lives willingly for God, he dies in obedience to God. He remains active throughout. He is not a victim, helpless in the face of death. The relationship of trust is not broken at the moment of death. Even as we live to the Lord, so we die to the Lord. Life and death are determined by God, and the believer's response to life and death is positive. Both involve an active surrender to God; neither is characterized by absolute autonomy. Everything is "unto the Lord." By the same token there is no despair because of the darkness; I deny the darkness and abandon myself with trust into the hands of God. With Jesus Christ the Christian learns to say, "Father, into thy hands I commit my spirit!" The moment of death is one of trust and commitment, of spiritual activity.

Has not the Christian learned all along to die with Christ? Is this not the secret of overcoming the natural, instinctive fear and anguish? Christ left us a pattern that we should follow.

The specific context of this admonition refers to the passion and death of Christ (I Peter 2:18-25). Indeed, Christ was obedient unto death, even death on a cross, and we are admonished to have the mind of Christ (Phil. 2:8, 5). Christ endured death in the right spirit and with the right attitude.

The Christian does not "perish like a beast," but follows the pattern of Christ. Active trust at the moment of death transfigures the experience of dying.

But, as was pointed out before, it would be an oversimplification to speak of THE Christian attitude toward death, to quote a biblical text in the assumption that it solves the problem of death or elucidates the mystery of existence. We must do justice to the wealth of biblical material.

The Christian must confront death — I must face death. I shall die and I must avoid false optimism or exaggerated pessimism. The latter would ruin the joyful experience of life. Actually the Christian can delight in life more than anyone else because he knows that God has given us all things richly to enjoy. No longer enslaved by the fear of death (Heb. 2:14,15), the Christian can experience life with gladness; ultimate questions have already been faced, the assurance of divine forgiveness has been obtained, life has become harmonious. The relationship initiated by God is based on acceptance. A man responds to the love of God evidenced in Christ. A note of triumph appears. In Paul's succinct phrase, God is for us, not against us. God really cares. Now we can live in the assurance that nothing can separate us from God's love, "neither death, nor life . . . nor things present, nor things to come . . . nor anything else in all creation" (Rom. 8:31-39). This joyful confidence inspires life, motivates action, and sustains hope.

God is life. All false glorification of death is alien to Christianity. As Samuel Johnson said, "Christianity can teach us to die well, but not eagerly." Death is an enemy, "the last enemy." On the very first page of Scripture death is seen as punishment. The words "you shall die" are a divine threat. The early genealogies repeat continuously that so and so lived a certain number of years "and he died." The genealogies may hint that the individual dies but the race goes on, but this survival by proxy is small comfort. The fear of death casts a deep shadow over the pages of the Old Testament. Long life is seen as a divine blessing because "he who is joined with all the living has hope, for a living dog is better than a dead lion" (Eccl. 9:4). It remains true that "the dead do not praise the Lord" (Psalm 115:17) like the living. Shadows do not rise up to praise God (Psalm 88:10). With stark realism the prophet Isaiah speaks of maggots and worms in connection with death (Isaiah 14:11).

At the same time, death is not only seen as an event at the end of life. Weakness, sickness, even imprisonment and oppression, are but forerunners of death, part of its accoutrements. Every shadow, even darkness itself, is a messenger of the king of terrors. The power of death casts a shadow over all of life. The medieval saying, "In the midst of life we are surrounded by death," is a fit description of the Old Testament attitude. "We must all die, we are like water spilled on the ground" (II Sam. 14:14) — death is irrevocable. One of the most graphic descriptions of old age and death is found in Ecclesiastes 12:1-8, and the conclusion that in the light of growing decay "all is vanity" hardly comes as a surprise.

The same realism characterizes the New Testament, although hope is the dominant theme. The body of Lazarus, dead four days, "stinketh." There are no easy evasions or facile phrases. The Christian dies! Death has sometimes been defined as the separation of soul and body; at the moment of death the immortal soul leaves the body and moves closer to God. In spite of the elements of truth, this is hardly a biblical picture. It is certainly an inadequate definition — a description at best. It would be a cardinal error to suppose that the body is a hindrance to fellowship with God. If this were so, why hope for a resurrection body, a hope which pulsates throughout the New Testament. Matter does not *per se* stand in opposition to its Creator. The idea that I have my integrity as a thinking entity — without body — is not scriptural. Man is not pure spirit, temporarily and accidentally dwelling in a body. It is simply not true that at death the artisan lays aside his tool, that the sailor steps out of the boat and reaches the harbor. Death is not liberation from a dungeon, for the soul is not imprisoned in the body. The soul alone is not the "real man," unaffected by death. The view of Plato that man is uninvolved at the moment of death, a mere spectator, is not biblical.

Body and soul belong together. Their separation is neither fitting nor normal. The rupture is violent and involves the total man. In fact, the word "immortal" is not used in connection with the soul in the New Testament. The Greek word translated "immortal" occurs only a few times. It is used of God "who alone has immortality" (I Tim. 6:16) and of the incorruption of the resurrection body (I Cor. 15:53, 54). The biblical emphasis falls on resurrection!

At the moment of death the body is not simply discarded. It is part of man's nature, of his very being. Without the body the soul is "naked." The body is like a tent, wrote the tentmaker, and will perish. But Paul has the assurance that we will obtain a new, permanent body, a "building" as opposed to the temporary "tent." Changing the imagery, the apostle speaks of the new body as a garment to be put on in order not to be found "naked." No one wants to be "unclothed" (die). It would be so much better if, instead of being unclothed, we could be "further clothed"; in other words, if the heavenly body could simply be put on like an outer garment without the experience of death "so that what is mortal may be swallowed up by life" (II Cor. 5:1-4). This will be the experience of those who shall be alive at the return of the Lord. They shall be changed in the twinkling of an eye, and this perishable will put on the imperishable, the mortal will put on immortality, and death will be conquered (I Cor. 15:51 ff.). But although Paul would rather be "at home with the Lord," he is willing to carry out his responsibilities and to await the pleasure of the Lord, whether death or instant transformation. But the moment of death is sufficiently painful that Paul would rather not be unclothed, but be further clothed. The separation of soul and body is not the liberation of the soul, but an extremely painful rending asunder of what belongs together.

Along with the body, the soul is also affected. The soul is indestructible but not impassive or imperturbable. It is imperishable and incorruptible but linked to the body. In death the soul is violently severed from the body — but not from God. The union with God is indissoluble, the fellowship uninterrupted (God is life). "With thee is the fountain of life" (Psalm 36:9a); "even though I walk through the valley of the shadow of death, I fear no evil; for thou art with me" (Psalm 23:4).

The believer has already been assured of eternal life. This gift of the living God is not an infusion of vitality, but a continuous gift of grace from the fountain of life; it is life of a totally different quality. It is not merely received at the end of life, but is a present possession. The Christian is assured of eternal life and receives it by the grace of God here and now. Even if death casts a negative shadow over all of life, the gift of eternal life illuminates all of life and assures us of ultimate triumph.

As Christians we should avoid the false optimism which belittles death as well as the false pessimism which overlooks the possession of eternal life here and now.

All of life is a movement toward death, and in that sense we die daily. But although our outer nature is wasting away, our inner nature is renewed day by day (II Cor. 4:16). Just as walking is actually a kind of falling, though with every step we check our fall, so life itself is a matter of dying that is repeatedly held in check. But we also walk with God — or rather, he walks with us, even through the valley of the shadow of death. So Paul can exclaim triumphantly that God is for us, that nothing can separate us from his love. We therefore can conquer through him who loved us. The divine initiative is not frustrated. We remain linked with God in death. Soul and body may separate and suffer, but we will not be separated from God.

If death has lost its terror for the Christian, this is not because he is unaffected — the soul simply leaving an alien environment, but because we are assured of God's abiding love. In this sense Jesus Christ has "abolished death" and brought life and immortality (literally, incorruption) to light through the Gospel (II Tim. 1:10). As a power and principle death has literally become "inoperative." Darkness and death are no longer the controlling principles in the Christian life. The believer's future is controlled by God. Death has lost its sharpness, its sting (I Cor. 15:55). Elsewhere Paul develops this thought more fully, proclaiming clearly that death reaches all men because of sin (Rom. 5:12), that "by a man came death" (I Cor. 15:21). "The power of sin is the law" (I Cor. 15:56), for "apart from the law sin lies dead" (Rom. 7:8). The law — any law — forces evil to a state of crisis, compels the disease of the human heart to come into the open. Paul also observes that sin is not counted when there is no law (Rom. 7:8), but that death reigned long before Moses gave the law. He concludes that death has come upon mankind because of the fall. Ever since then man has transgressed the moral law, disobeyed conscience, and disregarded God. The law of Moses only brought the basic tendency out into the open and demonstrated with unshakable evidence that, confronted by the divine law, all men are found to be sinners. So the law pronounces all men guilty because all have sinned — and sin is the sting of death. Paul uses the image of a scorpion whose power and poison is in his sting. The bitterness of death is attributed to the power of sin. But we are not left helpless victims. Bodily death without the intervention of redemption would have been nothing but a curse and eternal ruin, but through redemption the death of the body becomes an invaluable blessing. Indeed, we attain to the resurrection through death and death alone. The body is raised in incorruption only

if there has been previous sowing in corruption. God gives us
the victory through Jesus Christ. This is not an appeal to the
subjective feelings of the believer, but simply a calling of attention to the divine initiative of grace. Christ has delivered men
from the condemnation of the law. Sin is forgiven because of
the propitiatory death of Christ, and sin and death have been
conquered in his resurrection. We are one with him. The
resurrection of Christ is the only hope of victory over death;
his victory becomes ours. The Christian no longer lives under
condemnation. Sin is forgiven. This is a gift of God. The believer, like all other men, dies, but the sting is now removed.
The victory over death is certain because the hope of the
resurrection is immediately related to life here and now. Hence
the last words of chapter 15: "Therefore, my beloved brethren,
be steadfast, immovable, always abounding in the work of the
Lord, knowing that in the Lord your labor is not in vain." Far
from being passive or indifferent to the affairs of this life, the
Christian remains active and is inspired by new enthusiasm in
the light of the joyous hope of a glorious resurrection.

If death casts a shadow over the entire life of man, hope
inspires the Christian to action now. It was corrosive doubt
which had unsettled the Corinthian church, resulting in indifference characterized by the maxim, "Let us eat and drink,
for tomorrow we die." True Christian hope does not diminish
a keen interest in this life nor focus exclusively on the life to
come. On the contrary, assurance of ultimate victory produces
an abounding or overflowing in the work of God, in whatever
pleases God and is ordained by him. The response of faith
receives the victory which God gives and translates hope into
activity. Some may die courageously who have steel and nerve
enough to dare anything. Skydivers and car racers, for example,
claim a certain ecstasy in the face of death, but this is a far cry
from the Christian victory. Even necessity can help us to face
the inevitable. Sometimes it is the agony of suspense which
makes danger dreadful, and once the inevitable appears one
can face it with desperate calm. This is quite another thing

from the victory proclaimed by Paul. Nothing in the world ever led man to real victory except faith in Jesus Christ.

"All things are yours," exclaims the apostle, including life and death (I Cor. 3:22). The Christian is not the plaything of anonymous forces controlling the world. Beyond genetic factors, sociological situations, and the bondage of circumstances seemingly in control of life and death, stands the living God. All things cooperate or work together for good. God's living, personal will makes everything work together for the good of the believer, who uses the varied circumstances of life like a sailor uses the wind. The Christian is emancipated from the bondage of circumstances because all things are his. So life is lived fully, freely, and joyfully; and even death, which seems to come like a conquering tyrant, becomes subservient. Life and *death* are ours on one condition — that we are Christ's. Then all things serve us, even death, because we have surrendered to Jesus Christ and responded to his love. Free from the bondage of "things," we can enjoy life thoroughly. Free from the fear of death, we can face dying with confidence. We are not defeated by life nor crushed by death. Everything serves us, all things belong to us — if we belong to Christ. Fate, chance, circumstances are not the dominant powers controlling life, inspiring fear, discouragement or despair. Behind all the events of life we know God to be in control. We commit ourselves to him in an obedience rooted in faith and love. The ultimate is a person, a God who cares and in whom we trust. The result is freedom to live and to die.

How different from those who all their lives are held in bondage to the fear of death (Heb. 2:15). Even the finest philosophic minds of ancient Greece could not escape its gloom. The religion of Egypt was obsessed with death. The quest for immortality inspired countless rituals and sumptuous temples. But the particular biblical treatise alluding to the fear of death is not addressed to the Greeks or Romans nor to the pagan world in general. The letter is written to the Hebrews, familiar with the Old Testament. Was their life also permeated by the fear of death?

It is remarkable how little the Old Testament has to say about life after death, hope, resurrection, and eternal life. The Sadducees accepted the validity of the written law (rejecting only traditional interpretations which were accepted by the Pharisees) and denied the resurrection and personal immortality. Paul, an ex-Pharisee, declared without hesitation that it was Jesus who had shed light on the topic of eternal life and incorruption (II Tim. 1:10). In this respect the contrast between the Old Testament and the New Testament is most striking. It is therefore not surprising that Judaism has relatively little to say about life after death. According to Abba Hillel Silver, "the Torah shows no interest in the career of the soul after death." Judaism is "primarily preoccupied with life, with man's life here on earth." He goes so far as to write that "one cannot escape the impression that the deviation toward eschatology represented a sharp departure from classical Judaism."[1] Faced with the fear of death and looking for answers which traditional Judaism did not furnish, popular Jewish imagination filled the void. Theories about life after death evolved complete with purgatory and descriptions of the abode of the blessed and the damned. The Hebrews too lived under the shadow of death. In fact, if the Old Testament was remarkably reticent about life after death, the gloom of death was sufficiently emphasized to give rise to many questions. Sheol, or the abode of the dead, was described as "the land of gloom and chaos, where light is as darkness" (Job 10:22). It seems that compared to the living, those in Sheol lived a shadowy and feeble existence. It was a "land of silence" (Psalm 94:17) or a "land of forgetfulness" (Psalm 88:12). No wonder the psalmist prayed, "Hear my prayer, O Lord, and give ear to my cry; hold not thy peace at my tears! For I am thy passing guest, a sojourner, like all my fathers. Look away from me, that I may know gladness, before I depart and be no more" (Psalm 39:12, 13).

Speculation about the dead abounded, and the fear of death reigned supreme. Was Sheol not a place where all relationships were cut off? "For Sheol cannot thank thee, death cannot praise thee" (Isaiah 38:18a). Hope occasionally illuminated life, and the poet exclaimed, "God will ransom my soul from the power of Sheol, for he will receive me" (Psalm 49:15). Fellowship would somehow remain unbroken in death. But perhaps these expressions are only aspirations of faith or momentary insights. There is no assurance based on God's certain promise. All nations — even the chosen nation — were subject to the fear of death. Then came Jesus. His life and proclamation, his death and resurrection, threw new light on life and death.

"Through death [Jesus] ... destroy[ed] him who has the power of death, that is, the devil, and deliver[ed] all those who through fear of death were subject to lifelong bondage" (Heb. 2:14, 15). The devil makes death subservient to his own purposes; it is his realm. Death as such is not part of the divine order. True, the devil cannot inflict death on his own authority because God is the master of life and death (Heb. 9:27); but the devil's sway is exercised in the realm of death. He is a murderer from the beginning (John 8:44) and leads men into sin and death. At the same time it is through death that the Christian reaches his ultimate destiny: a genuine reflection of the divine image in a spiritual body.

The power and fear of death is cancelled in Christ's death and resurrection. Through his death forgiveness is assured and sin is cancelled; the sting of death is removed. Through Christ's resurrection we are assured of resurrection and life in the presence of God.

Jesus came to destroy the works of the devil (I John 3:8) and has triumphed over his power at the cross (Col. 2:15), binding the strong man (Matt. 12:29), bruising the serpent's head. This victory will be fully manifested when death, the last enemy, is totally banished. But the Christian does not have to wait for this ultimate fulfillment; we are already delivered from the dominion of darkness and the fear of death. In death the believer does not come face to face with God's wrath, mediated by the devil. Sin is forgiven and Satan's power is broken. The redeemed person is free — free to enjoy life and to face death. God gives us richly and freely all things to enjoy (I Tim. 6:16). Life belongs to us (I Cor. 3:22). Fear has yielded to hope.

Christian hope must be distinguished sharply from a mere waiting. The characters in *Waiting for Godot* had no hope, but waited and meanwhile tried to hang themselves. They felt alone in the midst of nothingness and needed to find something to do in order to maintain the impression of existing. Such waiting is akin to despair. Without hope life is empty, meaningless, and a frightening void. The Christian is called to hope like Abraham who "in hope . . . believed against hope" (Rom. 4:18).

He who is joined with all the living has hope, but human expectation is usually disappointed because of the uncertainties surrounding us. In fact, the word "hope" seldom expresses more than a desire or a longing. Christian hope is different. It is accompanied by trust and attended by certainty. It is a forward look with conviction based on God's promises. It is an eager expectation of God's blessing. It is far more than aspiration. When Paul stated that the heathen lived "without hope" he certainly did not mean that they were devoid of aspiration, seeking, yearning, and desiring. But in the truest sense they were without hope because they lived without the ultimate assurance which can only come from God.

The gift of hope has accompanied mankind from the very beginning of history. The promise of a redeemer (Gen. 3:15) was fulfilled in Christ who is the center of our hope. Hope pierces through time. It is not technical; it is not interest in the *how*. According to Gabriel Marcel, "Hope and the calculating faculty of reason are essentially distinct and everything will be lost if we try to combine them."[2] He defines hope as "a knowing which outstrips the unknown — but it is knowing which excludes all presumption, a knowing accorded, granted, a knowing which may be a grace but it is in no degree a conquest."[3] True hope is indissolubly linked with humility. It is attached to the divine promise and heard in faith.

The case for hope is not based on a rational assessment. Hope is not based on shrewd calculation or clever planning. Hope furnishes a new sense of direction, an enormous impetus. Today's widespread despair is not a result of the intense pressure of reality, but of the absence of genuine hope. Old men no longer dream dreams and young men seldom see visions (Joel 2:28; cf. Acts 2:17-21) because the inspiration of the Spirit is missing.

But hope cannot be generated by command. It can only come to life if man rediscovers God and responds to him. Paul states bluntly that outside of the Christian world there is no hope (I Thess. 4:13), meaning no well-founded hope in connection with eternal life. At this point it would be easy to furnish more quotations from heathen philosophers preceding Paul or contemporary with him to illustrate the truth of the apostolic statement. Often cited is a second century papyrus: "I was sorry and wept over the departed one . . . all things whatever fitting I did . . . but nevertheless against such things one can do nothing. Therefore comfort ye one another." Philosophy offered little more. The Stoic showed no interest in the concept of hope. Others had their own dreams and aspirations, but their expectation was ill-founded.

Christian hope is anchored in God. He is the author of hope (Rom. 15:13). It is because of God's act through Jesus Christ that hope is possible. It is centered on the divine activity manifested in the resurrection of Christ (I Cor. 15). We have a living hope through the resurrection of Jesus Christ (I Peter 1:3). This hope implies confidence and is allied with patient waiting. Christian hope is not calculating or intelligent foresight, for hope that is seen is not hope (Rom. 8:24). True hope is rooted in God's grace (II Thess. 2:16) and produces joy because we are assured of sharing the glory of God (Rom. 5:2).

The glory of man was lost at the moment of the fall. His effort to attain glory is doomed to failure. Substitutes give no lasting satisfaction. The glory of power, money, position, or whatever else it may be, does not last. All our endeavors fall short of the glory which God can bestow (Rom. 3:23). Ultimately man will be glorified; we shall follow the steps of Jesus and through death reach resurrection and eternal glory. This hope is the "anchor of the soul" here and now in the midst of all change, and at the moment when we face the greatest change — death.

A great deal has been written about the rapid changes of society and the resulting uncertainties and rootlessness. Such studies usually overlook the large segments of the world's population where change is far less pronounced and where the same fear of death and alienation prevails. But, be that as it may, the Christian is far better equipped than most to confront radical change, even the final experience of total transformation. The Christian has already welcomed the most extreme transition, turning toward God! From here on in he remains open to God, flexible, adaptable. Throughout life the believer remains conscious of the fact that "a man's mind plans his way, but the Lord directs his steps" (Prov. 16:9). The most rigid plans are made "under God," who will correct and revise our projects and purposes and sometimes indicate a new direction. The believer remains flexible and knows that man proposes, but God disposes. All our deliberations are short-sighted; our calculations do not include every contingency. We make plans and abandon ourselves with joyful confidence to God. Changes are not resisted arrogantly. Humility leads to openness and receptivity. Throughout all the vicissitudes of life trust in God reigns supreme. The natural resistance to change, the fear of the one irrevocable change, is not characteristic of the believer. Until the very end he commits life and death unto the Lord.

Actually the changes which occur at death are not all negative. The end of physical life is also the moment of deliverance from all sin. The Christian subscribes to the words of Paul, "The wages of sin is death" (Rom. 6:23). Sin is a divisive factor. It separates man from God, alienates man from man, and produces chaos and disorder within man. It is true that the Christian is assured of forgiveness and that, in fact, he has become a new creation. The most radical change has taken place. Life is no longer determined by sin, but by resistance to sin. A new power is at work. The vital center is renewed. But if darkness no longer rules, if the enemy no longer occupies the citadel, he still remains encamped about it and renews his assaults. In principle the Christian belongs to the realm of life and light, but at the same time sin is still a real factor and clings to the very best. Motivation is imperfect and even the best actions are only acceptable to God through the mediation of Jesus Christ (I Peter 2:5). No one is free from sin in this life.

But God is light, and without holiness no one shall see the Lord (Heb. 12:14). It is the pure in heart who shall see God (Matt. 5:8). Since no one dies in perfect purity and holiness one must either assume a period of cleansing after death (the concept of Purgatory) or believe that at the moment of death all sin is obliterated, that the time of probation is ended and sin is removed completely along with temptation. The inclination to sin is ended; holiness is confirmed. Now death appears in a new light. In the very moment when the power of death is most keenly felt, the power of sin is permanently broken and both sin and death overcome. A change — be it ever so painful in itself — which leads to such a glorious result shall not be feared. Fellowship with God is now unclouded. We shall always be "with Christ."

Paul puts it quite simply when he speaks of his own death as a "departure" (Phil. 1:23). The root meaning of the Greek word used here is quite interesting. It refers to an "unloosening" and is used of a prisoner who is released. Death is an experience of freedom! But the same word would be used by the farmer for the "unyoking" of an ox. Death is the end of all toil, a moment of rest. The philosopher using the same word would refer to the "unravelling" of a problem. Death is the beginning of illumination, when we shall know far beyond anything we have known so far. Finally, it is the word of a locksmith who "opens" the lock. Death is the penetration of a mystery. Faith is replaced by sight, aspiration by fulfillment. A new freedom breaks in, rest is undisturbed, illumination enjoyed, and new life received.

It is not surprising that Abraham, the man of faith and hope, was quite ready to die even though he did not possess the fulness of Christian hope. He died "full of years" (Gen. 25:8), satisfied with life. He had lived life to its fullness and was ready like a shock of grain that "comes up to the threshing floor in its season" (Job 5:26). This attitude may be easier for older people. Abraham lived 175 years!

The New Testament counterpart to Abraham is Simeon. He also was content to die. Having seen God's salvation, he was grateful for the divine permission at last to leave his post as the sentinel when the hour of his watch is over. "Now lettest thou thy servant depart in peace" (Luke 2:29). Peace in the prospect of death! The purpose of life had been fulfilled. Simeon recognized God's absolute right to keep him alive or to dispense with him as he willed. The word translated "Lord" is literally "despot." The emphasis falls on sovereignty, not slavery; and Simeon felt secure in God's hand. He possessed the peace of completeness, of hope fulfilled. This is not a false glorification of death, but one more truly Christian perspective. If union with God is one of the essential elements of life, death can be seen as the final unification. All obstacles to union with God are now removed. Death becomes the transfiguration of life and leads to a more complete and permanent union with God. Fear is expelled by love (not courage), because love unites. "There is no fear in love, but perfect love casts out fear" (I John 4:18).

At this point Christian thinking becomes child-like in its

simplicity. God really cares. We have this assurance through the life, death, and resurrection of Jesus Christ. I experience this love of God in forgiveness. In the very measure in which sin-consciousness prevails I gain a deeper awareness of the divine mercy. I respond to the initiative of God's love. As John put it, we love him because he first loved us. Love seeks union. Throughout life this love toward God becomes a powerful motivating factor. It flows from a deepening experience of God's forgiveness. "There is forgiveness with thee, that thou mayest be feared" (Psalm 130:4). Thus the fear or love of God is rooted in forgiveness. The experiences of life confirm on a practical basis the teaching of Scripture regarding the sinfulness of man. Increasing sin-consciousness creates a correspondingly increasing appreciation of God's grace. Life is lived in response to God's love, and death will finally unite us with the object of our love. Assured of acceptance of forgiveness, we can face death with equanimity and peace.

Regardless of all these practical and theological considerations, it remains that many Christians cannot face death without fear. Perhaps this is partly because the fear of death is seldom discussed in our churches. To admit to such fear might result in a loss of face; one might be considered unspiritual for harboring such thoughts. If this is the case, a deplorable atmosphere prevails fostering hypocrisy and a judgmental spirit. The church, of all places, should be the center of fellowship where openness prevails and anxieties can be shared.

The mere fact of being a Christian does not automatically remove the fear of death. But perhaps the greater concern is for the loss of those whom we deeply love. Although we may have learned to face our own death, that of others is a matter of deep concern. The problem assumes terrible dimensions when we are faced with the loss of someone in the prime of life. Of course Christians sorrow. Regardless of the assurance of life in all its fulness in the presence of God, Christians need comfort. It is also true that we do "not grieve as others do who have no hope" (I Thess. 4:13). We may not grieve in the same manner or to the same extent because of our hope, but the sorrow is genuine. The tragic dimensions of life are not obliterated for the Christian.

Despite everything that can be said from a Christian viewpoint, regarding death and life after death, the answers are always inadequate or else our capacity to embrace the divine answer is insufficient. Only perfect love casts out fear (I John 4:18), and our love is never perfect. Elements of fear remain, although love and fear are diametrically opposed. Fear is not expelled by courage but by love. Fear and love cannot coexist because love gives and shares in a spirit of self-surrender, whereas fear shrinks away in distrust and hides. It is impossible to approach God in love and to hide from him in fear at the same time. However, since faith and love in response to the divine initiative are always imperfect, the Christian cannot automatically expect to be delivered from all fear or anguish. A greater awareness of God's forgiving love and grace will gradually reduce fear and increasingly annihilate the natural darkness resulting from the fact of death — whether my own or the death of someone else.

Perhaps death becomes particularly painful when it involves someone who seems never to have established a relationship with God through Christ. What God in his sovereign freedom and grace will do remains unknown to us. Many a comforting sermon has been based on the criminal on the cross who accepted the claims of Christ at the moment of death. On the other hand, attention should also be focused on the other criminal who in the face of certain death and in the presence of Christ remained obdurate. It matters little in this context whether the criminals were revolutionaries or brigands, prepared by their Jewish faith or remote from all religious concerns. We know nothing about their specific knowledge or background. Nevertheless, the interesting implications raised in connection with their death should not be overlooked.

Again and again we hear it reported that people who have been rescued from the imminent threat of death have, before losing consciousness, reviewed their entire life. In an article entitled "The Pleasures of Dying," *Time* magazine reported the experience of a skydiver whose parachutes failed to open. He hit the ground at an estimated 60 m.p.h. but escaped with minor injuries. Later he told reporters what the plunge had been like: "I screamed. I knew I was dead and that my life had ended. All my past life flashed before my eyes, it really did. I saw my mother's face, all the homes I've lived in, the military academy I attended, the faces of friends, everything." [4] Psychiatrists call it the moment of transcendence or ecstasy; philosophers indicate that the soul or the power of the mind is over and beyond time. To some extent we all experience this in dreams lasting a few seconds which deal with events covering years. How many units of measurable time are needed for a decision? What happens when all of life unrolls with perfect clarity before the mind's eye! Can a loving impulse be measured with a chronometer? If man has this God-given faculty, surely it represents a last invitation and opportunity to take a step toward God. All human judgment is premature, and as Christians we can only rejoice in God's sovereign freedom and love.

No one single answer will dispel all doubt and eliminate all fear, but from a Christian perspective we can certainly say with David:

As for me I shall behold thy face in righteousness;
when I awake, I shall be satisfied with beholding thy form.
(Psalm 17:15)

VIII
SUICIDE

More than half a million people a year commit suicide. In the United States alone some 25,000 each year are known to take their own lives. The true figure may well be twice as high since many suicides are listed as natural or accidental death out of deference to the family or because of inadequate investigation. In addition, there are at least 200,000 attempted but unsuccessful suicides per year.

It is not surprising that a new science has flourished: suicidology. There are a large number of suicide prevention centers in the United States, and hundreds of books on the topic have been published. All this has resulted in an enormous accumulation of data. It may indeed be interesting to know that dentistry and psychiatry lead all professions in the number of suicides among their members, that women attempt suicide three times as often as men but fail far more frequently, that Hungary leads the world in the national suicide rate, and that the Golden Gate Bridge is a favorite spot (although rarely on sunny days). In fact, the entire bridge is now closely scrutinized by closed-circuit television, and a special squad will rush out if anyone manifests abnormal behavior. San Francisco has the dubious distinction of surpassing the national average by 2.5 percent, and perhaps this is not surprising when other facts and figures are considered. It so happens that San Francisco leads the nation in per capita consumption of alcohol, and the two facts are probably interrelated; both are symptoms of a deeper malaise. The population of San Francisco consists very largely of elderly persons, homosexuals, and lonely people.

Two thirds of the residents are either single, separated, divorced, or widowed. Facts and figures can sometimes illuminate the problem and point to solutions.

It is estimated that in the United States as many as 1000 young people between the ages of fourteen and twenty-one take their own lives. Death by suicide is more prevalent on campus (especially Harvard, Yale, and Berkeley) than among the general population. Among young urban Negroes suicide is a serious problem. In New York, for example, suicide is twice as frequent among Negro men between twenty and thirty-five as among white men in the same age bracket. On the other hand, after the age of forty-five suicide among whites rises to a higher level.

Myths about suicide abound despite all the published material. It is not limited to the uneducated, the poor, the sick, minority groups, writers, or the insane. It is certainly not true that those who talk about suicide will seldom take their lives. In fact, two thirds of all suicides have previously tried to kill themselves. It is true that there is always an ambivalence: an intense desire to live along with an urge to die.

Suicide is no respecter of income or social status. It matters little whether the name is Cleopatra, Ernest Hemingway, George Sanders, Marilyn Monroe, Vincent Van Gogh, Ernest Bellows, or Joe Doe. People from all backgrounds take their lives. In some cultures, such as Japan, suicide has been acceptable, but by and large it has always been considered a crime. From the legal standpoint it concerns the State because it devalues life as much as any form of murder, and because suicide attempts often imperil the lives of other people. In many countries one can be imprisoned for attempting suicide. Some claim that this prohibition is a Christian superstition in a post-Christian age. It remains to be seen whether we have entered the much touted "post-Christian" era; nevertheless, a "superstition" which keeps a person alive is certainly of the better kind.

Why do people commit suicide? Naturally much attention has been focused on this question and various answers have been given. To single out one motive is hardly reasonable. Human beings are complex and many different motives enter into play. Perhaps no totally satisfactory answer can be given because each case is different. Besides, too many suicides defy investigation because no clue is left behind.

If some people who are without hope are driven to suicide, others, also without hope, continue to live and accept the situation as a challenge. Boredom, depression, a sense of alienation, shame, real or imagined guilt — these and other factors are hardly the exclusive property of those who commit suicide. Are people who kill themselves suffering more acutely because circumstances are indeed desperate, or is it rather that others seemingly in similar or worse circumstances simply refuse this easy exit? How can suffering be measured? Is the inner response to the external situation the key factor? Or does heredity play a major role? How can one determine the intensity of feeling or the degree of selfishness involved?

The various reasons to explain some suicides are not satisfactory; the problems exist to some extent in all persons. The difference might be one of degree or intensity, a highly personal area where measurements elude the investigator. The question persists: why do some people take their lives while others do not, although to the outsider their circumstances are quite similar? Of course, the same question has been raised more broadly in the area of national survival and development. Why is it indeed that the Eskimos failed to respond to the challenge of their environment and produced instead an "arrested civilization," to use the language of Toynbee? On the other hand the Jews, dispersed and persecuted, have met the challenge successfully. At what point in the experience of a nation or of an individual does the challenge become unbearable?

Sociologists have proposed different theories, although there are admittedly almost as many viewpoints as researchers. Facts and figures are of little help. How indeed can one explain why the national suicide rate in Denmark is twice as high as that in the United States or Great Britain? Why do Norway, Holland, Ireland, and Spain have low suicide rates, whereas Switzerland, Austria, and Denmark have high rates? The United States is in the middle range of national suicide statistics, but suicide remains the tenth most common cause of death for all Americans.

Freud formulated the theory that suicide is a form of aggression which, instead of being directed toward other people, is turned against oneself. But this theory hardly squares with the fact that many countries are high in suicides and yet low in homicides (Denmark) or high in assassinations but low in suicides (Italy). The idea that it is an inverted homicide, the outgrowth of an unconscious desire to kill someone else, has largely been forsaken. In this area Freud is no longer popular.

Actually, the psychodynamics of suicide vary from culture to culture. Within primitive and civilized cultures there is striking variation in its meaning, significance, and frequency. Dr. E. J. Kempf distinguishes eight different causes of suicide:
  — religious devotion and loyalty which compel devotees to follow a king, chief, or husband to the grave;
  — fanatical experiments due to faith in life after death;
  — as an alternative to execution for military dishonor;
  — the preference of self-inflicted death to one by torture;
  — to avoid becoming a burden on others;
  — as an impulsive act, perhaps dictated by unusual pressures;
  — guilt and shame;
  — revenge, compelled by brooding, feelings of injury, or a conviction of the futility of love.

Other researchers have assumed four basic causes:
  — impulsive anger; extreme disappointment or frustration;
  — the feeling that life is no longer worth living;
  — a very serious illness;
  — revenge.

All theories refer again and again to shame, guilt, feelings of inferiority, and alienation. Human beings have an innate need for response, recognition, and security. But these needs cannot be gratified without emotional contact. A sense of isolation destroys this possibility, and extreme loneliness coupled with a sense of uselessness leads to self-destruction.

Alienation often flows from a feeling of inferiority which is in turn caused by a sense of guilt ("I did something wrong") or shame ("I don't measure up to the standard set by myself or others"). It is quite obvious that the causes to which suicide is commonly attributed, such as alcoholism, drug addiction, unemployment, domestic problems, insanity, morbid fears, ill health, and desire for revenge, are only significant when it is seen *how* these elements are part and parcel of the life of the individual, how they are interwoven with many other patterns in his life. Needless to say, these factors are extremely difficult to determine. In addition, several researchers admit that between 62 and 85 per cent of those who commit suicide do so "for reasons unknown" — or at any rate the reasons are not made known, although they are perhaps known to close friends or relatives. Nevertheless, sociologists and other researchers persist in listing numerous factors contributing to suicide.

It may come as a shock to many readers, but Christians are not immune to suicide. There are too many well-documented cases to the contrary. Christians are not exempt from the pressures of life, and in spite of their faith — and obviously in some instances because of their faith — they cannot always overcome the temptation to end their life. It has indeed been suggested that there is no valid reason for Christians not to commit suicide since they are assured of eternal life and look forward to the resurrection. But it could and should be argued that the very idea of continued existence after death makes this life meaningful. The Christian view should therefore act as a powerful antidote to suicide. This life is a preparation for eternity and therefore renders this life precious and significant — although not necessarily or inevitably pleasurable.

The Bible mentions several cases of suicide, and interestingly enough, without adverse comment. In the New Testament the case of Judas is most famous. Peter observes that Judas "went to his own place," a nice euphemism for Hell. However, Peter did not declare that Judas went into eternal darkness because of his suicide. It is enough in this connection to mention Judas' betrayal of the Master and to recall the words of Christ regarding him, "Woe to that man by whom the Son of man is betrayed! It would have been better for that man if he had not been born" (Matt. 26:24).

The Old Testament mentions several cases:

- ABIMELECH was mortally wounded and asked his armorbearer to slay him with the sword (Judges 9:54);
- SAMSON destroyed himself and in the process took the lives of his enemies. In the New Testament he is listed among the heroes of faith (Heb. 11:32);
- SAUL took his own life rather than be tortured by his enemies. His armor-bearer followed his example (I Sam. 31:4-5);
- AHITHOPHEL hanged himself when his counsel was rejected (II Sam. 17:23).

It is obviously a mistake to assume that every case of suicide is evidence of lack of faith (see the case of Samson). Appearances are deceptive. An outsider viewing Christ on the cross might have assumed that he was a criminal who deserved his sentence. It is easy to draw premature and incorrect conclusions.

The Christian Church has always and unequivocally condemned suicide. It is a transgression of the command "Thou shalt not kill" and a sin against nature and charity. Thomas Aquinas stressed this point, explaining that suicide does injury to the community and assumes God's right to give life and to take it away. He emphasized three basic Christian concepts: human life is sacred; submission to God is essential; the moment of death is important. It has been argued that in most cases suicide is compulsive rather than rational and therefore does not fall within the province of Christian theology or ethics.

Outside the Christian tradition it is more difficult to establish reasons for not committing suicide. In the opening statement of Camus' *The Myth of Sisyphus,* the author writes, "There is only one truly serious philosophic problem, the problem of suicide." Why should one endeavor to prolong life? If life is absurd, irrational, and more miserable than happy, why not end it all? Why endure? Stoics like Marcus Aurelius and Seneca advocated and committed suicide. The thoroughgoing atheist would find it difficult to advance sufficient reasons against it.

Hamlet evaluates the possibility of suicide in his famous soliloquy and concludes that

> The dread of something after death,
> The undiscover'd country from whose bourn
> No traveller returns, puzzles the will
> And makes us rather bear those ills we have
> Than fly to others that we know not of.

The argument needs no elaboration. Based on rational evidence, one can at best (or worst) be agnostic but never be absolutely certain about life after death. It was Jesus Christ who shed light on death and immortality! Outside of the Gospel, unaided by revelation, man can only remain uncertain and refuse to gamble since "dreams may come" and death may not "end at all." But side from the element of uncertainty, there are additional reasons why suicide is condemned.

People often attempt suicide for reasons which are erroneous. One is reminded of the Philippian jailer who was ready to take his life because he thought all the prisoners had escaped. Paul did not deliver a sermon regarding the sacredness of human life but simply assured him that they were all present. There is a time for practical, direct statement and another time for reflective consideration. Paul pointed out that the real problem of the jailer lay in a totally different area. A study conducted in London determined that physical illness is the principal cause of 18 percent of all suicides. Often the fear of incurable disease (especially cancer) is the main reason. Yet post mortem examinations have revealed that treatment had been successful in many cases and that there was no recurrence. How often is despair ill-founded and our analysis of the situation too short-sighted.

It is surprising how a seemingly simple gesture or insignificant event can dispel the notion of suicide. Malcolm Muggeridge in *Jesus Rediscovered* writes:

> There was one point in my life when I decided to kill myself, and I swam out to sea, resolved for a variety of reasons that I didn't want to live anymore. Partly it was a mood of deep depression, and partly actual difficulties. I swam out to sea until I felt myself sinking; you get a strange kind of sleepiness that afflicts you, as if you were just about to fall into a deep sleep. I thought that I would take one last look at the coast, and that would be the end. I saw the lights along the coast; and I suddenly realized that that was my home, the earth— the earth, my home, and that I must stay on the earth because I belonged there until my life had run its course. Then somehow, I don't know how, I swam back.[1]

Tolstoy also describes how at one point he was rescued from suicide:

> "I remember," he says, "one day in early spring. I was alone in the forest, lending my ear to its mysterious noises. I listened, and my thought went back to what for these three years it always was busy with—the quest of God. But the idea of him, I said, how did I ever come by the idea?
>
> "And again there arose in me, with this thought, glad aspirations towards life. Everything in me awoke and received a meaning. . . . Why do I look farther? a voice within me asked. He is there: he, without whom one cannot live. To acknowledge God and to live are one and the same thing. God is what life is. Well, then! live, seek God, and there will be no life without him. . . .

"After this, things cleared up within me and about me better than ever, and the light has never wholly died away. I was saved from suicide. Just how or when the change took place I cannot tell. But as insensibly and gradually as the force of life had been annulled within me, and I had reached my moral death-bed, just as gradually and imperceptibly did the energy of life come back. And what was strange was that this energy that came back was nothing new. It was my ancient juvenile force of faith, the belief that the whole purpose of my life was to be *better*. I gave up the life of the conventional world, recognizing it to be no life, but a parody on life, which its superfluities simply keep us from comprehending,"—and Tolstoy thereupon embraced the life of the peasants, and has felt right and happy, or at least relatively so, ever since.[2]

Hermann Hesse speaks of "periods of despair" when he felt like a lost pilgrim who had reached the extreme edge of the world, "and there was nothing left for me to do but to satisfy my last desire: to let myself fall from the edge of the world into the void — to death."[3] Gradually however this suicidal impulse vanished, and he learned to accept these hours of despair even as he learned to accept acute physical pain: "One endures it, complainingly or defiantly; one feels it swell and increase, and sometimes there is a raging or mocking curiosity as to how much further it can go, to what extent the pain can still increase."[4] Elsewhere Hesse concludes that, regardless of suffering and despair, a great many suicides have derived an uncommon strength from the thought that the door to escape is always open. But the hero maintains throughout the secret hope that, regardless of the seeming madness and meaninglessness, ultimately God's presence will be revealed to him and order rise out of chaos.

Obviously Muggeridge, Tolstoy, and Hesse have made significant contributions to their contemporaries and subsequent generations. They still had a great deal to give when they contemplated suicide, and their lives gained new meaning through service to others. Not every one who contemplates suicide and despairs of the futility of life will ultimately have the same influence, but countless numbers of those who toyed with suicide and finally rejected the thought, or even attempted it and failed, have subsequently lived meaningful lives. Since the future is uncertain and our perspective always limited, how foolish it is to cut off the future irrevocably.

In the final analysis suicide is always an act of cowardice, an attempt to escape regardless of the cost involved to others. Suicide does in fact cast a shadow over the lives of others, and no one has the right to escape his own difficulties by burdening other people. Suicide is therefore the act of a self-centered person, unwilling to accept the hardships which are an integral part of life.

Death never gives meaning to life, according to Sartre; on the contrary, it deprives life of significance. Death does not solve any problem. Sartre would say this of death through suicide. Only the future can give meaning to life, and since there is no future in my suicide, life remains totally undetermined and immersed in absurdity.

Paul rejects an atomistic view of society. No one has a right to live for himself. If a person had this right, he could do anything he cared to with his own life, including destroying it. But life is a gift of God, and we do not have proprietary rights. Jesus Christ is Lord of the dead and the living. But in addition to this argument, suicide is also condemned because man does not live in total isolation. It is significant that in Romans 14:7, 8 Paul uses "we," a word expressing solidarity. Elsewhere Paul develops the idea of the body to express the concept of solidarity. If I kill myself I do not only harm myself, but I injure all of life. The entire body suffers when one member suffers or dies. Paul strikes a nice balance between extreme individualism on the one hand and collectivism on the other. All of life is related in all its dimensions. The service of God, a relationship on a vertical level, cannot be severed from the horizontal relationship with men. No one lives or dies to himself.

Many attempted suicides are only thinly disguised forms of tyranny. The suicidal threat is made without the slightest intention of carrying it out, but only as a means of bending the will of others and bringing them into subjection. The message is clear in its brutality: If you do not comply with my wishes my blood shall be on your head. This is a contemptible method of gaining control over others, the last resort of a weak, egocentric individual. To yield to this extreme pressure leads to enslavement. The refusal to yield demands considerable strength of character and may leave doubts in the mind of the person. If the suicide is actually carried out or at least attempted (and this possibility always exists), feelings of guilt may overshadow all else. This situation is intolerable and indicative of serious personality problems which need professional help to be resolved.

The problem is that every threat of suicide is not empty. It is simply not true that those who talk about it actually never take their lives. But together with such direct statements one should watch for other signs. There are indeed warning signs which can give a clue. The following list is not exhaustive, but it may be helpful:

— insomnia;
— neglect of personal appearance;
— prolonged depression;
— disposing of prized possessions;
— suicide threats and notes.

Obviously, many of these symptoms are interrelated. Depression usually manifests itself through an unkempt appearance, a withdrawn attitude, lack of sleep and appetite. The inability to concentrate, constant fatigue, and general apathy are all marks of the loss of a positive self-image. These are danger signs and should be taken seriously.

Regardless of all the arguments which can be advanced against suicide, it may not be possible to dissuade the person contemplating it. His is an emotional decision based on non-rational factors. To show genuine concern for the person may be more helpful than a battery of arguments. It may also be necessary to invoke the help of specialists, to contact a suicide prevention center, or to secure guidance from more experienced people to deal with the person considering suicide* Christian love will inspire the necessary sensitivity and tact in dealing with suicidal tendencies in other people and inspire the practical steps which may be necessary to counteract them.

* Between 150 and 200 suicide prevention centers are in operation in the United States. They are primarily staffed with nonprofessional volunteers, using the telephone as a basic tool. It would be excellent if churches could get involved in this type of ministry and create crisis intervention centers. For additional insight into the problem see: "Suicide Prevention in the Seventies," published by the National Institute of Mental Health, 5600 Fishers Lane, Rockville, Md. 20852.

IX
FUNERAL CUSTOMS

Funeral customs have varied tremendously in different cultures across the centuries. Some have buried their dead, while others have preferred cremation or in some cases exposure of the corpse. The Egyptian *Book of the Dead* advocates a totally different ritual from the Tibetan *Book of the Dead* regarding the shape of the grave, the position of the corpse, the coffin, the funeral ceremonies, the time of the funeral, and the mourning and purification ceremonies.

The ancient biblical tradition was relatively simple. It was customary to kiss the dead (Gen. 50:1) and to close their eyes (Gen. 46:4). Inhumation followed death almost immediately because the heat would hasten decomposition. The corpse was not embalmed; mummification was an Egyptian custom (Gen. 50:2, 26). Instead of a coffin, the corpse was simply placed on a bier. Only after the Babylonian exile did caskets come into use, but only with the wealthy.

Royal funerals were more magnificent. Spices were burned (Jer. 34:5) and special lamentations were offered by those "skilled in lamentations" (Amos 5:16; cf. Jer. 9:17). "They laid [King Asa] on a bier which had been filled with various kind of spices prepared by the perfumer's art; and they made a very great fire in his honor" (II Chron. 16:14). Subsequently he was buried in a tomb which he had hewn out for himself in Jerusalem. The main external signs of mourning consisted of the tearing of garments, girding with sackcloth, putting ashes on the head, lying on the ground, or fasting. Cremation was not customary among the ancient Hebrews except for those convicted of serious crime (Lev. 20:14). The body of Saul was burned, and the bones buried under a tamarisk (I Sam. 31:12, 13). The case of Saul was unusual; the Philistines had mutilated the corpse and left it exposed for some days, and it was no doubt in a state of putrefaction (I Sam. 31:8ff.).

Another instance of cremation is found in Amos 6:9, 10: "And if ten men remain in one house, they shall die. And when a man's kinsman, he who burns him, shall take him up to bring the bones out of the house, and shall say to him who is in the innermost parts of the house, 'Is there still anyone with you?' he shall say, 'No'; and he shall say, 'Hush! We must not mention the name of the LORD.' " The original text is uncertain. The words "He who burns him" could also be translated "he who makes a burning for him" (RSV margin) and refer to the person burning spices. On the other hand it is quite possible that pestilence made cremation necessary in order to avoid pollution. In fact, in case of pestilence the multitude of corpses ("If ten men remain in one house, they shall die") might not be disposed of any other way.

Cremation was introduced in the Mediterranean basin in the days of Homer (850 B.C.?). The first reference to it appears in the *Iliad* in connection with the death of Patroclus. The poet explains that the purpose of the new custom was to carry the bones of the fallen warrior back to his native land (*Iliad* 23:110ff.; cf. 7:331).

The ancient practices had hardly changed by New Testament times. The corpse was placed on a bier (Luke 7:12), hands and feet bound with bandages and the face wrapped with a cloth (John 11:44). A procession of friends and mourners would accompany the bier (Luke 7:12). Hired mourners and no less than two flute players lamented the dead. Whenever the cortege stopped between the house and the cemetery, the mourners would break out in rythmic chants and exclamations both of sorrow and praise for the dead. It was a sacred duty to join the cortege even if it interrupted the study of the Torah. Interestingly enough, the cortege did not stop on the way to the cemetery for the funeral of a woman.

Normally several persons relayed each other in the sacred duty of carrying the corpse.

According to the New Testament, the body of Jesus was anointed with sweet smelling ointment (Mark 16:1) and wrapped in a clean linen shroud (Matt. 27:59).

The early Christians developed extremely simple customs partly because of poverty but more especially because of the hope of the resurrection. The body was washed (Acts 9:37), anointed with myrrh, and then wrapped in linen. It was then buried in a tomb cut out of a rock or in a cave. A brief description ("In Peace") or a Christian symbol (a palmbranch or fish) marked the place.

Eusebius, describing a pestilence which occurred in Alexandria around 261 A.D., relates how the Christians took the bodies of the dead believers, "closed their eyes and their mouths, bore them away on their shoulders and laid them out; and they clung to them and embraced them; and they prepared them suitably with washings and garments" (*Ecclesiastical History* VII, 22). Gradually funerals became more ornate. The body of Constantine was placed in a gold coffin, enveloped in a covering of purple and surrounded by candles. The most elaborate funeral ceremonies were concluded with a military salute (*Life of Constantine*, 60, 66-72).

Chrysostom (A.D. 390) found it necessary to speak out against the professional mourners who wailed, groaned, and howled, tearing their hair and shrieking violently (*Homilies on Hebrews*, 4). Although the funeral customs of the early Christians varied from country to country, they were marked by simplicity and respect for the body.

Tertullian (A.D. 145-220) opposed cremation, calling it a cruel custom because the body is undeserving of an end which is inflicted upon murderers (*A Treatise on the Soul*, ch. 51). Similarly Minucius Felix (A.D. 210) praised the Christian custom of burying in the earth (*The Octavius*, ch. 34). Here the appeal is to an ancient custom rather than to dogma.

Hardly anyone would advocate a return to early Christian

funeral customs. They too were, in part, influenced by a specific culture and are not normative for ours. Still, one characteristic is noticeable — simplicity. Unfortunately, this is no longer the case in North America. Funerals have become elaborate and costly. According to an article in the Chicago *Daily News* (Oct. 1, 1970), "Basic funeral and cemetery costs in Chicago total about $1,800. But it's easy to spend $3000 to $4000." Inflation has certainly not helped matters. According to recently released figures, the average funeral expense in America totals $983. This figure does not include vault, cremation or crematorium expenses, the monument or marker, or miscellaneous items such as honoraria for the clergyman, flowers, additional transportation charges, burial clothing, or newspaper notices. In addition, grave space ranges anywhere from $75 to $350. This, of course, does not include the opening and closing of the grave. Cremation ranges from $35 to $150, and the urn runs from $50 to $250.

There are approximately 37,000 cemeteries in the United States occupying roughly two million acres. Mausoleums are "in," and some have been valued at two million dollars. There is a mausoleum in Nashville twenty stories high and estimated at 12 million dollars. It will contain 130,000 crypts, lying seven deep, all made from three-inch-thick, steel-reinforced concrete. The higher the crypt the lower the cost! The special coffin costs only about $500 and is available in Early American, French Provincial, and Mediterranean style.

When the influence of the church weakens, the undertaker assumes a quasi-priestly role. When the concept of resurrection is lost, death has to be masked or hidden. The euphemisms are multiplied, and illusions and superficialities abound. Most people are not even aware of the fact that in most states embalming is not required by law, so long as burial takes place within twenty-four hours and the body is not shipped out of state. Only 5 percent of the dead are cremated at this point. It is interesting to note here that the Vatican lifted the ban on cremation in 1964. The method of disposing of the body should balance aspects of reverance for the body with practical considerations of hygiene.

The National Association of Funeral Directors stresses the idea of the "body present." After carefully pointing out that "what remains is not that living person," we are also reminded that we always remember persons "in terms of their physical being — their body." Therefore, with the body present "the loved one can be viewed." But it is hardly correct to equate the loved one with the body. We are also reminded that the preparation of the body — and, if necessary, restoration through cosmetics — provides an acceptable image of the deceased. The words "acceptable image" actually mean that the effects of pain or of possible disfigurement are removed cosmetically. The stark realism of death is minimized, and yet we are told that viewing the body helps children understand the real meaning of death. Actually, the reality of death is camouflaged.

It is indeed necessary for children to gain insight into the fact and meaning of death, but not from the presence of the restored body. It would be far better if terminal patients could die at home rather than in hospitals. In Chicago, for instance, only 9.7 percent die at home. It would certainly be preferable for the terminal patient to be surrounded by his own family instead of dying in an alien world.

Since there are no explicit biblical teachings regarding funeral customs, one can only appeal to broad principles such as simplicity, dignity, and respect. In this respect most funerals leave much to be desired; it is high time for Christians to review customs and cost, stressing the note of simplicity and the resurrection hope.

It might be practical to describe in the will how the funeral should be carried out, giving specific attention to the viewing of the body and its mode of disposal. This takes a considerable burden from the survivors, who are responsible for the arrangements. At such a highly emotional time people will not necessarily make the most rational decisions on the details of the funeral. All too often feelings of guilt or social considerations motivate decisions which cannot be justified on the basis of Christian ethics. Specific directions in the will obviate such problems, and the very fact of making a will helps one to face the reality of death. In this context the joyful hope of resurrection should receive its full due and guide Christian action.

NOTES

CHAPTER 2

1. Bernard Ramm, "A Christian Definition of Death," *Journal of the American Scientific Affiliation* 25 (June, 1973): 58.
2. Quoted from "Death with Dignity," *Hearings Before the Committee on Aging*, part 2 (Washington, D.C., U.S. Senate, 92nd Congress, 2nd Session, August 8, 1972), p. 64.
3. Quoted from Jacques Choron, *Death and Modern Man* (New York: Collier, 1972), p. 4.

CHAPTER 3

1. John Hinton, *Dying* (Baltimore: Penguin Books, 1968), p. 100.
2. David Cole Gordon, *Overcoming the Fear of Death* (Baltimore: Penguin Books, 1972), pp. 14, 15, 107, 115.
3. *See* Walter Kaufman, *From Shakespeare to Existentialism* (Boston: Beacon Press, 1959), p. 64.

CHAPTER 4

1. David Cole Gordon, *Overcoming the Fear of Death*, p. 20.
2. Herman Feifel, ed., *The Meaning of Death* (New York: McGraw-Hill, 1959), p. 71.

CHAPTER 6

1. D. T. Suzuki, *Mysticism: Christian and Buddhist* (New York: Harper & Row, 1971), pp. 132, 133.

CHAPTER 7

1. Abba Hillel Silver, *Where Judaism Differed* (New York: Macmillan, 1972), p. 312 ff.
2. Gabriel Marcel, *Homo Viator* (New York: Harper Torch, 1962),
3. Ibid., p. 10.
4. "The Pleasures of Dying," *Time* 100 (Dec. 4, 1972): 62.

CHAPTER 8

1. Malcolm Muggeridge, *Jesus Rediscovered* (London: Fontana Books, 1969), pp. 187, 188.
2. Quoted from William James, *The Varieties of Religious Experience* (New York: Collier, 1968), p. 157.
3. Hermann Hesse, *The Journey to the East*, tr. by Hilda Rosher (London: P. Owens, 1956), pp. 77, 78. *38 126000*
4. Ibid.